**A GIFT FOR**

_____

**FROM**

_____

**DATE**

_____

# THE POWER IN

### 100 WAYS TO TAP INTO THE COURAGE TO TRUST GOD'S PLAN OVER FEAR, WORRY, AND DOUBT

## SARAH JAKES ROBERTS

*The Power in Surrender*

© 2026 Sarah Jakes Roberts

Content in this devotional has been adapted from *Power Moves* (W Publishing, 2024) and messages by Sarah Jakes Roberts.

All rights reserved. No portion of this book may be reproduced, stored in a retrieval system, or transmitted in any form or by any means—electronic, mechanical, photocopy, recording, scanning, or other—except for brief quotations in critical reviews or articles, without the prior written permission of the publisher.

Published by Thomas Nelson, 501 Nelson Place, Nashville, TN 37214, USA. Thomas Nelson is a registered trademark of HarperCollins Christian Publishing, Inc.

The author is represented by the Dupree Miller Agency.

Thomas Nelson titles may be purchased in bulk for educational, business, fundraising, or sales promotional use. For information, please email SpecialMarkets@ ThomasNelson.com.

Unless otherwise noted, Scripture quotations are from the New King James Version®. Copyright © 1982 by Thomas Nelson. Used by permission. All rights reserved.

Scripture quotations marked ESV are from the ESV® Bible (The Holy Bible, English Standard Version®). Copyright © 2001 by Crossway, a publishing ministry of Good News Publishers. All rights reserved.

Scripture quotations marked KJV are from the King James Version. Public domain.

Scripture quotations marked NIV are from the Holy Bible, New International Version®, NIV®. Copyright © 1973, 1978, 1984, 2011 by Biblica, Inc.® Used by permission of Zondervan. All rights reserved worldwide. www.zondervan.com. The "NIV" and "New International Version" are trademarks registered in the United States Patent and Trademark Office by Biblica, Inc.®

Scripture quotations marked NLT are from the Holy Bible, New Living Translation. Copyright © 1996, 2004, 2015 by Tyndale House Foundation. Used by permission of Tyndale House Publishers, Carol Stream, Illinois 60188. All rights reserved.

Any internet addresses, phone numbers, or company or product information printed in this book are offered as a resource and are not intended in any way to be or to imply an endorsement by Thomas Nelson, nor does Thomas Nelson vouch for the existence, content, or services of these sites, phone numbers, companies, or products beyond the life of this book.

Without limiting the exclusive rights of any author, contributor or the publisher of this publication, any unauthorized use of this publication to train generative artificial intelligence (AI) technologies is expressly prohibited. HarperCollins also exercise their rights under Article 4(3) of the Digital Single Market Directive 2019/790 and expressly reserve this publication from the text and data mining exception.

HarperCollins Publishers, Macken House, 39/40 Mayor Street Upper, Dublin 1, D01 C9W8, Ireland (https://www.harpercollins.com)

Cover design: MAC Creative
Interior design: Kristy Edwards

ISBN 978-1-4002-3692-3 (HC)
ISBN 978-1-4002-3695-4 (audiobook)
ISBN 978-1-4002-3691-6 (eBook)

*Printed in Malaysia*

25 26 27 28 29 VPM 10 9 8 7 6 5 4 3 2 1

# Contents

1: Power Flow . . . . . . . . . . . . . . . . . . . . . . . . . . . . 6

2: Divine DNA . . . . . . . . . . . . . . . . . . . . . . . . . . . . 8

3: Check Your Gas Tank . . . . . . . . . . . . . . . . . . . . 10

4: Open to Change . . . . . . . . . . . . . . . . . . . . . . . 12

5: What Do You Want? . . . . . . . . . . . . . . . . . . . . 14

6: What Was Left Behind . . . . . . . . . . . . . . . . . . 16

7: God's Vision for My Values . . . . . . . . . . . . . . . 18

8: New Programming . . . . . . . . . . . . . . . . . . . . . 20

9: Moving with Confidence . . . . . . . . . . . . . . . . 22

10: Make Way for Growth . . . . . . . . . . . . . . . . . . 24

11: Even the Messes . . . . . . . . . . . . . . . . . . . . . . . 26

12: Defy the System . . . . . . . . . . . . . . . . . . . . . . . 28

13: Both-And . . . . . . . . . . . . . . . . . . . . . . . . . . . . . 30

14: Limiting Beliefs . . . . . . . . . . . . . . . . . . . . . . . 32

15: God Hunger . . . . . . . . . . . . . . . . . . . . . . . . . . 34

16: Grace and Self-Compassion . . . . . . . . . . . . . . . . . . . 36
17: Heaven Invading Earth . . . . . . . . . . . . . . . . . . . . . . . 38
18: From Preparation to Utilization . . . . . . . . . . . . . 40
19: Shame's Power Broken . . . . . . . . . . . . . . . . . . . . . . . 42
20: The Jagged Edges . . . . . . . . . . . . . . . . . . . . . . . . . . . 44
21: Living a Fruitful Life . . . . . . . . . . . . . . . . . . . . . . . . 46
22: A Solid Base . . . . . . . . . . . . . . . . . . . . . . . . . . . . . . . 48
23: Fill an Empty Place . . . . . . . . . . . . . . . . . . . . . . . . . 50
24: Present and Engaged . . . . . . . . . . . . . . . . . . . . . . . 52
25: Power at Rest . . . . . . . . . . . . . . . . . . . . . . . . . . . . . . 54
26: Space for Recovery . . . . . . . . . . . . . . . . . . . . . . . . . 56
27: Room for Restoration . . . . . . . . . . . . . . . . . . . . . . . 58
28: A Force Among Forces . . . . . . . . . . . . . . . . . . . . . . 60
29: Holy Rhythm . . . . . . . . . . . . . . . . . . . . . . . . . . . . . . . 62
30: Controlling the Self . . . . . . . . . . . . . . . . . . . . . . . . 64
31: Beyond Envy . . . . . . . . . . . . . . . . . . . . . . . . . . . . . . . 66
32: False Confidence . . . . . . . . . . . . . . . . . . . . . . . . . . . 68
33: We Are Not Islands . . . . . . . . . . . . . . . . . . . . . . . . . 70
34: Joining Forces . . . . . . . . . . . . . . . . . . . . . . . . . . . . . 72
35: No Need to Isolate . . . . . . . . . . . . . . . . . . . . . . . . . 74
36: Unnatural Trust . . . . . . . . . . . . . . . . . . . . . . . . . . . . 76
37: Rushing Stream . . . . . . . . . . . . . . . . . . . . . . . . . . . . 78
38: Searching in the Dark . . . . . . . . . . . . . . . . . . . . . . 80
39: Bridge to a Miracle . . . . . . . . . . . . . . . . . . . . . . . . . 82
40: Reframe That Complaining . . . . . . . . . . . . . . . . . . 84

41: Flowing with Others . . . . . . . . . . . . . . . . . . . . . . . . 86
42: Proactive Communication . . . . . . . . . . . . . . . . . . . . 88
43: Grace to Survive . . . . . . . . . . . . . . . . . . . . . . . . . . . 90
44: On Assignment . . . . . . . . . . . . . . . . . . . . . . . . . . . . 92
45: Willing to Risk It All . . . . . . . . . . . . . . . . . . . . . . . . 94
46: My Weight to Carry . . . . . . . . . . . . . . . . . . . . . . . . . 96
47: Present and Open . . . . . . . . . . . . . . . . . . . . . . . . . . 98
48: Taking Responsibility . . . . . . . . . . . . . . . . . . . . . . 100
49: Taking Feedback . . . . . . . . . . . . . . . . . . . . . . . . . . 102
50: Active Accountability . . . . . . . . . . . . . . . . . . . . . . 104
51: Strength in Our Weakness . . . . . . . . . . . . . . . . . . . 106
52: What We Impart . . . . . . . . . . . . . . . . . . . . . . . . . . 108
53: Power in Proximity . . . . . . . . . . . . . . . . . . . . . . . . 110
54: Give Freely . . . . . . . . . . . . . . . . . . . . . . . . . . . . . . 112
55: Sowing Generously . . . . . . . . . . . . . . . . . . . . . . . . 114
56: What's the Root? . . . . . . . . . . . . . . . . . . . . . . . . . . 116
57: Stepping into the Moment . . . . . . . . . . . . . . . . . . 118
58: Let That Breath Out . . . . . . . . . . . . . . . . . . . . . . . 120
59: A Place of Increase . . . . . . . . . . . . . . . . . . . . . . . . 122
60: Increase in Disguise . . . . . . . . . . . . . . . . . . . . . . . 124
61: Best-Laid Plans . . . . . . . . . . . . . . . . . . . . . . . . . . . 126
62: The Issue with Surrender . . . . . . . . . . . . . . . . . . . 128
63: Fresh Faith . . . . . . . . . . . . . . . . . . . . . . . . . . . . . . 130
64: Grieve, Then Believe . . . . . . . . . . . . . . . . . . . . . . 132
65: Worth the Grief . . . . . . . . . . . . . . . . . . . . . . . . . . 134

66: These Dry Bones . . . . . . . . . . . . . . . . . . . . . . . . . . 136

67: This World Is Not My Home . . . . . . . . . . . . . . . . . 138

68: Made Holy . . . . . . . . . . . . . . . . . . . . . . . . . . . . . . . 140

69: Remember God's Holiness . . . . . . . . . . . . . . . . . . 142

70: Buried Alive . . . . . . . . . . . . . . . . . . . . . . . . . . . . . 144

71: Conflicted but Still Listening . . . . . . . . . . . . . . . . 146

72: Cemented by Maybe . . . . . . . . . . . . . . . . . . . . . . 148

73: Claim Your Holy Identity . . . . . . . . . . . . . . . . . . . 150

74: The Power to Pivot . . . . . . . . . . . . . . . . . . . . . . . 152

75: Silent Transition of Power . . . . . . . . . . . . . . . . . . 154

76: Intersection of Lost and Found . . . . . . . . . . . . . . 156

77: Don't Look Back . . . . . . . . . . . . . . . . . . . . . . . . . 158

78: Make the Investment . . . . . . . . . . . . . . . . . . . . . 160

79: Until It's Good . . . . . . . . . . . . . . . . . . . . . . . . . . . 162

80: Mark the Spot . . . . . . . . . . . . . . . . . . . . . . . . . . . 164

81: Context Matters . . . . . . . . . . . . . . . . . . . . . . . . . 166

82: Unfazed by the Dark . . . . . . . . . . . . . . . . . . . . . . 168

83: Death by Deception . . . . . . . . . . . . . . . . . . . . . . 170

84: An Inside Job . . . . . . . . . . . . . . . . . . . . . . . . . . . . 172

85: Believe His Narrative . . . . . . . . . . . . . . . . . . . . . . 174

86: Enough, As Is . . . . . . . . . . . . . . . . . . . . . . . . . . . . 176

87: Praying Power . . . . . . . . . . . . . . . . . . . . . . . . . . . 178

88: Position for Expansion . . . . . . . . . . . . . . . . . . . . . 180

89: Uproot It . . . . . . . . . . . . . . . . . . . . . . . . . . . . . . . 182

90: Unfiltered . . . . . . . . . . . . . . . . . . . . . . . . . . . . . . 184

91: Trust the Game Plan .......................... 186
92: Unsuspected Partner......................... 188
93: Make the Decision ........................... 190
94: Power over the Enemy........................ 192
95: Rough Draft ................................. 194
96: God's Flexibility ............................. 196
97: Powerful Confrontation ...................... 198
98: Who Are You? ............................... 200
99: Two Things Can Be True .................... 202
100: Finish Strong .............................. 204

*About the Author*..................................... 207

## 1  *Power Flow*

The Spirit of God, who raised Jesus from the dead, lives in you. And just as God raised Christ Jesus from the dead, he will give life to your mortal bodies by this same Spirit living within you.

ROMANS 8:11 NLT

**A FEW MONTHS INTO LIVING IN OUR NEW HOME, MY HUS-** band and I were ready to unwind with an episode of our favorite show. I grabbed the remote and pointed it at the television. Nothing happened. I exchanged the batteries in the remote with fresh batteries. I extended my arm and pressed Power again. The black screen didn't budge.

I unplugged the TV and then plugged it back in. Pressed the button on the actual device. Nothing. As a last resort, I grabbed my husband's clippers and tested the outlet. The clippers began to hum as soon as I clicked them on.

Through a process of elimination, I could confidently say that the problem wasn't the remote or the outlet. The problem was happening inside the television. The power was flowing, but something internally was keeping the TV from converting the power into function.

If you've ever felt incapable of demonstrating confidence, then you may be more like the busted TV than you realize. If we could peek inside your thoughts in those moments, we'd see that you're not without ideas to contribute or a perspective to share, but you can't figure out how to get what's in you out of you.

Fortunately, there's a secret advantage to being like that television that should give you a sense of relief. It would have been a major headache if there were faulty wires in the wall or some other electrical issue hindering the flow of power. But the television had access to power. The issue was with the device.

Can I offer you a gift that can help to unblock some of what you're experiencing? Right now, in this very moment, power is on and flowing in your direction. Undoubtedly, there may be something blocking the flow, but doesn't it feel good to know that power is closer than it appears?

There is something about the way you are presently wired that is keeping the power you have access to from converting into the confident, resilient, and bold person you desire to become. In this devotional, I'm going to help you untangle the wires that make you feel like you're short-circuiting when you should be moving with intentionality, authority, and confidence.

Until we discover what beliefs, or lack thereof, are clamping your flow, you will have temporary bursts of power but nothing sustainable. Your situation may seem dire and a shift in your environment may absolutely be necessary, but nothing changes until you change. You are in your way. That may seem like a strong statement, but I will unpack it with you. With each turn of a page, you will feel yourself reclaiming strength, confidence, creativity, and vision. You're going to break through what has limited you—armed with the power to never be limited again. You are not meant to be a broken fixture in your world that resembles something familiar and useful but is just taking up space. You're a force in the making.

## LAY IT DOWN

Even when everything in my life says otherwise, power is flowing in my direction.

# 2 Divine DNA

> Put on your new nature, and be renewed as you learn to know your Creator and become like him.
>
> COLOSSIANS 3:10 NLT

**THE CREATION STORY IN GENESIS 1 TELLS US THAT WHEN** God created man and woman, He made them in His own image. Given that God does not have physical form, the only image we could possibly bear that resembles our Creator must be an inner image—our spirits. I'll be the first to say that my insides look nothing like God's. Instead, my insides are like a melting pot bearing the image of all the prayers, fears, hopes, memories, dreams, and nagging insecurities that I have.

I've met enough people to know that my insides are not the only messy interiors on this planet. Yours are too. All of us are messy in some way, but not all of us embark on the journey of trusting that there is power in our mess.

When one person cleans up even one corner of their messy life, they break a link on the chain that has prohibited generations from experiencing the freedom that comes with growing in power.

God envisioned a human experience that didn't require inner work before outer impact. When He created humanity, He released us to be a force instantaneously. He used big words like *subdue* and *dominion*. "And God blessed them. And God said to them, 'Be fruitful and multiply and fill the earth and subdue it, and have dominion over the fish of the sea and over the birds of the heavens and over every living thing that moves on the earth'" (Genesis 1:28 ESV).

Why would God have used such powerful words unless He

knew in His plan that Adam and Eve could access the power necessary to fulfill that charge? When God gave them the command, He didn't require them to work through their nerves, doubts, abandonment issues, or perfectionism.

Those are all things you and I confront now before we can even consider God's perfect plan for our imperfect lives. You know why God did not need to untangle Adam and Eve's thoughts from His thoughts? Because they were meant to be so perfectly made in God's image that their thoughts were His thoughts. Their ways were His way. The DNA of their insides bore the fingerprints of God's power.

If we're self-aware, when we embrace the notion that our insides were meant to bear the image of God's character, it can be discouraging. Because we know how far off we are from being anything like God. The distance, though expansive, is not insurmountable. There have been moments in my life when I knew for sure that my heart was perfectly aligned with God's, and change happened in me and through me. In those moments, I knew that the Holy Spirit made up the difference between my doubt and God's abundance.

Each day grants us another opportunity to get closer to reflecting God's image. It doesn't matter what decisions you made yesterday. If you stay alive for one minute past this moment, that's one minute you can use to bear God's image and reflect His heart to every person you encounter.

## LAY IT DOWN

Today, God invites me to join Him on the journey of becoming more and more like Him.

# 3 Check Your Gas Tank

Each time he said, "My grace is all you need. My power works best in weakness." So now I am glad to boast about my weaknesses, so that the power of Christ can work through me.

2 CORINTHIANS 12:9 NLT

**IMAGINE WITH ME YOU'RE STANDING IN AN EMPTY PARK-**ing lot with reserved spaces. You can't tell what each space is labeled, but each time a new expression of your identity is added, a car pulls into a spot. Eventually, you see that there are spots labeled *child*, *friend*, *sibling*, *partner*, *leader*, *student*, *entrepreneur*, or *colleague*. Each spot with its own car. When you are navigating the responsibilities of your life, you're moving from one vehicle to the next.

You leave your leadership car, which is full of gas, and hop into your friendship vehicle, only to see it's out of gas. You had enough power to galvanize your team toward success, but you don't have the power to admit to your friend that you haven't found a way to introduce who you're becoming into your dynamic. You feel like a bad person because you can't be the kind of friend that you know she needs. In reality, you're neither a bad person nor a bad friend. You've simply run out of the capacity to be the friend she once knew.

Often we chalk our awkward feelings to something we can overpower; eventually, it breeds annoyance and resentment in an area where we once had intimacy and joy. When the mere thought of having an encounter with someone deflates you, take the time to work through how your connection with them requires that you disconnect from yourself. Pushing past those moments is how we give license for their expectations of us to be more powerful than our authenticity.

The need to be refueled in one space does not equate to an overall powerless existence. Additionally, avoiding where we feel powerless doesn't make it go away. Most of the time we're all navigating the reality that we're strong in one space but weak in another. That's why being powerless can be so debilitating. When you have experienced your ability to execute and deliver in one space but have been stagnant in another, it's frustrating. Too often we settle for functioning only in expressions where power comes easily and refueling is not a mystery. Not this time though. If you can consume affirmations, take a nap, read a scripture, unplug, sign up for adventure, or view a message to get motivated, then you should feel comfort. You have found a formula that fills you again once power is decreasing.

I like the parking lot analogy because it speaks to the multidimensional expressions we possess as humans, but it also liberates us from feeling like we're struggling in every area of our lives. When you consider all the reserved spots you occupy as one person with many expressions and check the power tank on each of them, you may learn that you're not depleted everywhere. Instead, the areas where you're feeling least fulfilled are affecting you so significantly that they're detracting from courage and confidence in other places.

This is an opportunity for you to examine what's happening in those areas that is blocking the power of Christ from flowing to the place you need it the most. God's power is not reserved exclusively for accomplishing impossible tasks. It can also give you wisdom, patience, self-control, and strategy for the areas where you're feeling powerful.

## LAY IT DOWN

I am not stuck on empty. All the resources I need for refueling are available to me.

# 4 Open to Change

As you therefore have received Christ Jesus the Lord, so walk in Him, rooted and built up in Him and established in the faith, as you have been taught, abounding in it with thanksgiving.

COLOSSIANS 2:6–7

**ARE YOU LETTING THINGS THAT YOU HAVE THE AUTHORITY** to control rob you of power? It's easy to think about the big areas that we want to change, but what about the small drains in our lives? The actions and assumptions that poke holes and make way for slow leaks? I have felt powerless before in saving money, losing weight, participating in functions that I did not want to attend, condoning offensive behavior, or allowing someone to blatantly lie in an effort to keep the peace. I'd told myself that I was incapable of controlling the scenario, but that was never true. I just gave my fear of change more power than my fear of things staying the same. I could have saved the money, but I didn't want my lifestyle to change. I could have lost the weight, but I didn't want my diet to change. I could have said no to the functions, but I didn't want my circle to think differently of me. The fear of change is no longer allowed to hold you hostage.

The more you're willing to open yourself up for change, the more capacity you have for power to flow through you. With God you change your way into power by modeling your life after Jesus. The disciples didn't just drop their fishing nets and receive power (Matthew 4:20). No, they had to walk *with* power before they could walk *in* power. In walking with Jesus, they were able to ask questions about what was happening in their spirits and perspectives that was prohibiting them from doing what Jesus did.

A long-lasting love becomes richer and more powerful not

because things stayed the same but because two people were able to stay connected throughout all the changes. A friendship that withstands seasons of career changes, relocations, new loves, heartbreaks, and all the other highs and lows of life is a relationship that did not require a person to stay the same in order to remain connected.

To be honest, the relationships that I distance myself from have more to do with the person staying the same than with the person changing. If you're in my life, I expect you to change and grow. When I witness my friends taking the awkward, uncomfortable path toward growth, it inspires me. Anyone who needs you to never change is requesting that you never discover who God has destined you to become.

I have moments when I'm like, "Man, God is so faithful!" and other moments when I'm like, "God, where are You?" It's not because God has changed His character, but because God has changed His expression. The most beautiful part of my story has been sitting back to watch and see how God is going to show up next in my life. I just have to remind myself to trust that my search for where or how God is moving will never be in vain.

Throughout the Bible we see how God changed His expression. Sometimes He spoke directly to His creation; other times He used nature to speak to humanity. Then we see Him move through prophet after prophet—still God, but a new expression. The same all-powerful God made you in His image. A simplified version of you will frustrate your insides because you were empowered for more. I'm not even talking about more material possessions, businesses, or resources. I am not suggesting you're empowered to get more. You, my friend, have been empowered to become more.

## LAY IT DOWN

Surrendered to God, I am able to do so much more than I can even comprehend.

# 5 *What Do You Want?*

Lord, all my desire is before You; and my sighing is not hidden from You.

PSALM 38:9

**YOU KNOW HOW YOU SEE SOMEONE DOING SOMETHING** totally amazing and think, *I could never do that*? We only think we can't do something when we don't have enough personal evidence of a *can't* becoming a *can*. At this point, I think my toxic trait is that I think I can do anything—and when I say *anything*, I mean anything! Build a house? If you give me a book or a YouTube video, I'll figure it out. I call it toxic because the house I build is more than likely going to collapse. But I cannot get out of my head the notion that if someone else has learned to do this, then I can use the mind God gave me to attempt to get it done myself. I've learned to do many things I never thought I'd be able to do, so I am no longer easily convinced that there's something I can't figure out. Nothing in my life changed until I stopped being *can't*-focused and instead became *can*-focused.

Maybe you've disguised your want behind a *can't*, but it all has the same sum: Your *can't* has more power than your want. You may be thinking something like, *Yeah, well, not everyone gets what they want*. You're right. But denying what you want means you can't present your truth to yourself, let alone God. If something you want is not aligned with what God has for you, He will teach you how not to want it any longer. God can't remove from your heart what you won't confess with your mouth.

Wanting the same thing as God places you and God on the same team. Another crazy possibility that you may have never considered is that God wants the same thing for you as you want for yourself. What if the thing you're denying that you want is actually the thing God has been waiting for you to want? There's a powerful transfer that takes place when we begin to want the same things as God. It is the only way we are able to truly tap into limitless power or ability for whatever circumstance we're facing.

So how do you know when you and God want the same things? It starts with having a mutual, agreed-upon goal. It's no different than being in a marriage or galvanizing individuals to become a collective. There may not be agreement on how something will be accomplished, but there must be agreement on what will be accomplished. The goal is for you to get to a place where what you want is for God to be glorified in every circumstance. When you begin to want the love, power, creativity, compassion, and overall character of God to be revealed in your life and through your life, you and God are on the same page.

There will be moments when you know exactly how to make that happen and then other seasons where you don't know where to start. I have learned that those are the moments when I must trust that God is working while I am waiting.

When you and God are on the same team, there will be times when you're on the bench and He's taking the lead. What a relief it is to know that power is not about feeling strong, intelligent, or full of wisdom and moving through life with grit. Power is about showing up as your true self even if that version of you is different from who you were yesterday, five years ago, or five minutes ago. When you practice showing up in your truth, it allows the Lord to lead you into perfect truth for your life.

## LAY IT DOWN

God cares about the things I desire, and He loves hearing my prayers.

## 6 What Was Left Behind

Give us this day our daily bread.

MATTHEW 6:11

**GOING THROUGH LIFE ON AUTOPILOT MAY FEEL LIKE IT** helps you have a steady flow of power, but I am beginning to believe it only guarantees that you have recycled power. Daily bread is available to us each day based on how we're feeling and what God knows we need, but we can't tap into the daily bread we need if we haven't taken the time to acknowledge our needs in the first place. It's time to give yourself permission to acknowledge where you have need. From that place of honesty, you're able to honor where you are and petition God to reveal where you should be. After spending a lifetime of denying or avoiding my truth in order to pursue acceptance, I've experienced liberation. There is power in being honest with yourself and then sharing that honesty in your relationships with God and others.

You may be wondering, *How do I embark on a journey of identifying what my needs are?* I downloaded a feelings wheel a few years ago because I recognized that my emotional vocabulary was limited. Sometimes it's not that you are actively avoiding how you feel or who you are, but that you've never been given the language to accurately identify and express yourself. My prayer life became much more intimate when I was able to connect the truth of what I was feeling by using specific words like *sorrowful, agitated, insignificant, hopeful, creative, valued,* and so many more.

You may feel powerless because you have spent more time denying your truth than you have doing the work to understand what rejection or awkwardness you are actively trying to avoid.

You probably know a few people who subscribe to the belief system that admitting you have needs won't change the fact that they can't be met, so it doesn't matter anyway. You might be one of them. If you've been alive for longer than twelve months, you are well aware that you don't always get what you want. Don't worry, I'm not about to tell you that the moment you identify what you want it will come into your life.

I'm offering you something much more meaningful—the opportunity not just to admit what you want but also to grieve the things you wanted but didn't get to have. Take this opportunity to invite God into a corner of your heart that you rarely visit so that you can release the frustration, anger, tears, and disappointment for not getting what you wanted. Then, because God loves you so much, He'll show you, in that very same space, what He offered you instead. If you can't admit that you wanted it but didn't get it, God can't show you how He made provision for the area where you experienced lack. Let that be your bread today.

Power is not just reserved for moving forward. Power is also able to go back and heal what you've tried to leave behind. One of the most widely quoted scriptures in the Bible is "I can do all things through Christ who strengthens me" (Philippians 4:13). The apostle who wrote this was not declaring that he could do whatever he wanted but acknowledging that with Christ there was no situation he could not survive.

## LAY IT DOWN

It's time for me to move from ignoring my disappointments to trusting God can handle the areas where I'm struggling.

# 7 God's Vision for My Values

> Be strong and of good courage; do not be afraid . . . for the LORD your God is with you wherever you go.
>
> JOSHUA 1:9

**I GREW UP IN CHURCH, AND I'LL BE THE FIRST TO ADMIT** that my Bible must have had melatonin in the pages because when I would open it up, I'd feel my eyes getting heavy and slumber falling on me. I had to be honest with myself about not knowing where to start with such a big book. I learned to overcome this hurdle by opening up my Bible and Google at the same time. I'd put in a simple search like "scripture about disappointment." Instantly, I could choose from pages of scriptures that spanned the Old and New Testaments. I'd skim through a few until one pricked my heart.

Then I would flip open my Bible and read the whole chapter of whichever scripture made my heart feel a little less achy. Searching for scriptures about courage, worry, doubt, heartbreak, or fear is how I began to tap into how God redirected what a person in a similar situation to mine should value.

What I loved about doing those searches was that most of the scriptures that came up were scriptures about God, Jesus, or the apostles professing what not to do and what to do instead. For instance, when Joshua was leading a generation of people who were finally entering a territory that was promised to them, God gave Joshua insight on His ultimate plan and how Joshua was to position himself for success. Joshua 1:6–7 says, "Be strong and of good courage, for to this people you shall divide as an inheritance the land which I swore to their fathers to give them. Only be strong and very courageous, that you may observe to do according to all the law which Moses My servant commanded you; do not turn from it to the right hand or to the left, that you may prosper wherever you go." Right before God gave Joshua this command, He let him know that one season had ended and a new season was beginning. Joshua, who was the assistant to the deceased leader, was now being positioned to take command. In order for him to effectively shift from servant to servant-leader, he would have to allow his values to shift as well.

All we know is that Joshua was a trusted, loyal servant to the previous leader, which means he must have placed value on serving that leader with intention and dedication. Now that he was leading, God was letting Joshua know that his success as a leader would depend on him being strong. As part of his new value system, he could no longer value being an obedient servant to a man but rather a relentless leader who fastened onto the promise that God had given.

Unpacking the book of Joshua reveals that the territory promised to Joshua's people would be contested many times. There were even moments when the people he'd been tasked to lead were frustrated and overwhelmed by the magnitude of their opposition. If Joshua hadn't leaned into God's promise, he could not teach those he was influencing to do the same. Alternatively, if he had not demonstrated strength, his values could have been swayed, and he would have surrendered to the whims of the people instead of leading them with confidence.

If you truly believe that God is all-knowing and all-powerful, then when you lean into His vision for your values, you are being positioned for what will grant you access to the version of yourself that has the most power for the task at hand.

## LAY IT DOWN

What I value determines how I show up, and how I show up determines what doors are open to me.

# 8 *New Programming*

Out of the abundance of the heart the mouth speaks.

MATTHEW 12:34

**ONE WOULD FIND IT STRANGE IF A PERSON MADE THE** same meal every day . . . until they looked in the pantry and realized that the person was simply preparing a meal based off the available ingredients. If you have ever found yourself hungry for a version of yourself that you can envision but not access, you're not alone.

When you take the time to cultivate the core values that align with the most powerful version of who you are, you are changing your appetite. But when you get ready to live those values out, you have to change what's in your pantry. Otherwise, you'll have an appetite for a version of yourself that you're not equipped to produce. You have to do the work of implementing systems that make your core values easily attainable.

You may value self-care, but your programming is not currently set up to allow you to make room for yourself. Instead of breaking out of the system, you might become resentful and frustrated.

I know firsthand how challenging it is to channel what you value into your actions. Your systems are wired in your brain, but your core values exist in your heart. Without the proper system in place, what's in our hearts won't show up in our actions.

The desire to change the results that you're getting in life requires you to do more than refine your values. You must examine your inner systems for potential viruses that sabotage the transformation you want to experience.

Nothing is wrong with having a system. It's not possible to

show up in all the ways you do without a framework that takes into account the limits and boundaries you need to feel stable and productive, and being a healthy contributor to your community is not possible without being properly programmed. However, systems that have not been interrogated become viruses that snuff out our fires before they can even blaze. This internal malware spreads inadequacy, fear, doubt, and worry that quenches your potential and blocks your blessings.

You may have been programmed to fear scarcity, laziness, or lack, but now your body is deteriorating, and you're tired before the day begins because you feel guilty when you rest. Maybe you've been programmed to please others before you consider yourself, and now you feel resentful when your needs go unmet.

I'm praying that God will give you the desire to question the way you are programmed. Maybe you already know you've been programmed to play it small for far too long. It's time for you to break covenant with the wiring that has comforted you so you can receive the update that God went to great lengths to make sure you could receive.

## LAY IT DOWN

God has provided what I need to break out of old systems and access His vision of who I'm becoming.

# 9 Moving with Confidence

Let us lay aside every weight, and the sin which so easily ensnares us, and let us run with endurance the race that is set before us.

HEBREWS 12:1

**ONE OF MY FAVORITE STORIES IN THE BIBLE IS WHEN** Jesus was left behind in Jerusalem. His mother, Mary, and earthly father, Joseph, finally found Him after three days, and Jesus' response has always stuck with me. "He said to them, 'Why did you seek Me? Did you not know that I must be about My Father's business?' But they did not understand the statement which He spoke to them" (Luke 2:49–50).

Jesus was confused they were expecting human behavior from someone who was programmed for divinity. Mary and Joseph did not just leave Jerusalem with their child; they left with an awareness of how He was wired, which would serve them in raising Him. Sometimes the greatest gift you can give the people you're connected to is an insight into how you are programmed.

You are not supposed to be governed by your programming; you're supposed to be governing your programming. You may be holding yourself accountable for your inability to overcome a particularly burdensome circumstance in your life, but perhaps your time would be better spent understanding the malware that created the circumstance in the first place. Too often we look at the outcomes of our lives at face value. We penalize ourselves for our inability to make tough decisions. The fault is not our own. Underneath the surface of whatever or whomever you're trying to break free from is a virus that has distorted your confidence.

Part of the reason Genesis 3 had generational implications

is not just because the man and woman ate from the tree and sin entered the world; it's that sin's entrance also inserted a virus that seeks for you to arrive at a state of shame, humiliation, pain, fear, and rejection. In this system we constantly question God's intentions. It's a system of pain and distrust, a system that has made it more difficult than necessary to experience uninhibited connection with God. It is still functioning today because viruses like this are difficult to eradicate. It is so powerful that it doesn't even have to rely on a specific person to stay alive.

You must be willing to actively consider whether your system is outdated for where you're headed and whether your environment is nimble enough to withstand the discomfort of your introducing a new system.

You could be frustrated because yesterday's system has become today's restriction. What if the systems we once needed are the systems that are now oppressing? Is it possible that the system that once served you well has now become an enemy to your destiny?

It's important to understand the system that seduces you to power down when you should be turning up. Being armed with this knowledge allows you to better recognize what you're up against when you set out to overpower what has been obstructing you from moving with confidence.

## LAY IT DOWN

I do not have to accept any programming that draws me away from the love of God or the love that God has placed in my life.

## 10 Make Way for Growth

> See, I am doing a new thing! Now it springs up; do you not perceive it?
>
> ISAIAH 43:19 NIV

**CONSIDER THE RECURRING MOMENTS THROUGHOUT YOUR** day when you feel your power is being zapped. Maybe you commit to introducing a new habit into your schedule, but the moment you get stressed, you abandon the new habit and fall back into negative behavior. Maybe it's not that you have poor willpower, but that you have a system of stress in your life that prohibits you from achieving your desired goal.

Have you ever set out to begin creating social media content, but the moment it was time for you to press Record, you couldn't bring yourself to step into the moment? Maybe you actually manage to create the content, but the idea of sharing it makes you send it to the archives before it can be published. What about attempting to have a difficult conversation about your changing needs with someone you hold dear? Do you clear your throat to speak up and then make an excuse to avoid going deep?

Those are some examples I hear often, but if they aren't striking anything for you, then let's try another angle. If it's too difficult to understand your own system, zoom out and consider the system of your family. If you have not made a conscious effort to undo the negative systems that shaped you, then the systems that exist in your family are likely showing up in your life. If you have made a decision to do things differently and still can't define your system, I'll pose one simple question to you: What do you intentionally do differently to ensure that you do not repeat what you experienced? Somewhere in there lies your system.

Imagine that this system of yours is a printer that marks each sheet with odd ink marks. No matter what you print, the same marks appear on the paper. Eventually, you'd open up the printer to try to figure out what's happening inside the machine.

Upon opening the door of the printer, you'd see how many parts are working together to print your one sheet. The ink cartridges, printhead, adjuster lever, control panel, edge guides, and more all work together in a system. You may not know how the system works, but that doesn't keep you from examining what each part does.

If your life is constantly marked with the same outcomes, then the only way to find out what's going on is to open up and see how you're receiving, processing, and responding to the demands of your life.

If you're going to move in power, it will disrupt your world, but it does not have to destroy it. I am asking you to trust that the environment assigned to bring out your destiny cannot function with a diminished expression of who you are.

I'll be honest and admit that a more expanded you will rub some people the wrong way, but there's a possibility that the rubbing is actually massaging their ability to accommodate you. May God grant you the courage to be patient with those who need time to adjust and to distance yourself from those who will destroy your growth.

## LAY IT DOWN

A healthy disruption can create more intimacy and trust than staying in the status quo.

## 11 Even the Messes

> I am persuaded that neither death nor life, nor angels nor principalities nor powers, nor things present nor things to come, nor height nor depth, nor any other created thing, shall be able to separate us from the love of God which is in Christ Jesus our Lord.
>
> ROMANS 8:38–39

**THE SYSTEMS THAT LEAVE YOU STAGNANT AND ASHAMED** are rendered powerless only when a stronger, more powerful belief is introduced. That new belief introduces an opportunity for a healthier, more powerful system to emerge. Failure to take advantage of that opportunity occurs because our new belief must compete with our old system. God loves me whether I am in a relationship with someone or not. God loves me whether I am successful professionally or not. God loves me whether other people like me or not. These statements are opportunities to believe differently, but until our choices reflect what we believe, we will not experience change.

The belief that I am loved, valued, and worthy of maximizing my life is not one that I grasped with ease. It is a truth that required me to see beyond what I think about my messy insides and to dare to believe that where I see mess, God sees material. Romans 8:28 says, "And we know that all things work together for good to those who love God, to those who are the called according to His purpose."

It's a powerful scripture that has so much meat, but the word that stands out the most to me is *know*. Too many times we quote this scripture, replacing the word *know* with *think*, *wish*, or *hope*. There's something to be said about being in relationship with

God long enough that you move from the space of uncertainty about how things work together to a place of knowing.

I have learned that when God causes all things to work together, it's because God is so holy that even the messes I make along the way in the pursuit of His purpose cannot contaminate His holiness. That's not just my truth either. It's yours too. When I fall into the trap of inadequacy because of my negative belief system, I have to remind myself that God did not run out of grace when I messed up. When I trust that I am loved beyond measure, it breaks me out of the system that cripples me. There is a power waiting to be released in you that is rooted in the knowledge that you are inescapably loved, valued, seen, and adored.

If you are able to grasp this as truth, it will grant you the courage to change your mind about who you think you have to be in order to be palatable. Even more powerful is that it will change what you believe is possible.

Until you decide that you do not deserve the debilitating results that your system constantly produces, you cannot break out of your system. And you can't break out of your system if you don't acknowledge where you keep getting stuck.

Every time you make a choice opposite of what your negative systems dictate, you are serving notice to them that they no longer have power. If you want to know whether your system is healthy, you've got to look at the outcome you consistently produce. Even if the outcome is not what you desire, it can help you to better understand what system may be at play in your life.

## LAY IT DOWN

May God help me believe what He believes and rebuke what isn't from Him.

## 12 Defy the System

Do not conform to the pattern of this world, but be transformed by the renewing of your mind. Then you will be able to test and approve what God's will is—his good, pleasing and perfect will.

ROMANS 12:2 NIV

**I WANT TO BROADEN YOUR PERSPECTIVE ON WHAT YOU** need at this stage of your life. You don't just need a different outcome. You need a system rooted in love, compassion, worthiness, and the pursuit of heaven touching earth through you. I'll be honest and let you know that heaven doesn't touch earth through anyone who hasn't first faced off with hell.

The worst thing you can do when you've gone through hell and back is to repeat the same cycles and habits that bought the ticket to struggle in the first place. There is an authority that comes with surviving that must be enacted so that you no longer live trapped.

The old system doesn't relent because you wake up one day and say the season is over. No, you get a revelation, and when that revelation becomes consistent with your declaration and presentation, you will experience transformation. It's beyond being viewed differently because you put on a power suit so that others treat you with esteem. Real transformation is when what's taken place inside you becomes so evident that the external must adjust.

The negative thought process that has left you feeling like a shell of who you think you have the potential to become is operating as designed. It's the same old system that started in the garden of Eden. The template for that system was formed in darkness and seared as an imprint on humanity the moment

Adam ate from the tree, but it cannot have your future. It cannot have your community. It cannot have your children. The system has to end with you.

Since the system is functioning as designed, that means you have to get out of line. You must be willing to break free from the system that is trying to break you. If you don't break free from the system, you will never experience the power that is available to you. I know firsthand how difficult it is to break free. I also know the joy that awaits on the other side of freedom. Soon you will understand that the system wanted you to believe it was more powerful than you could ever be. The system is wrong.

The Old Testament tells the story of creation and follows God's relationship with His chosen people, the Jews. It also foreshadows the coming of the Anointed One, Christ, who would be their ultimate deliverer. The New Testament tells the story of the life and ministry of Jesus Christ, the Anointed One.

While some Jews did believe that Jesus was the Christ, many did not. Part of the reason many did not believe that He was the promised Messiah was that Jesus did not follow the rules of the Old Testament system. Certain customs were to be followed that Jesus frequently violated.

It's important to note that Jesus did not build His ministry on breaking rules and ruffling feathers. Jesus' mission was to restore creation with its Creator, God, by confronting and removing the generational curses of sin that divided us from God the moment that Adam ate from the forbidden tree.

For Jesus, the mission was worth defying the system. You can't withstand the consequences of defying a system without a mission that is more powerful than the possibility of retaliation.

## LAY IT DOWN

With God's help, the system ends with me.

## 13 Both-And

> If you remain silent at this time, relief and deliverance for the Jews will arise from another place, but you and your father's family will perish. And who knows but that you have come to your royal position for such a time as this?
>
> ESTHER 4:14 NIV

**ESTHER WAS A BEAUTIFUL YOUNG WOMAN WHO HAD** found a way to survive by denying her heritage as a Jew. Even when she was chosen to be the concubine of the Persian king, she maintained her disguise. It wasn't until she was made aware of the persecution of her people that she had some tough decisions to make. What I like about the story of Esther is that she did not immediately grab her cape and go running in the direction of destruction. She had legitimate concerns about the consequences of revealing her identity.

Sure, she'd found a way of existing that required her to not be authentic, but at least pretending promised her a sense of safety. Once Esther took the time to weigh her options, she chose to break out of the system that had offered her peace and to align with the path that would require her to stand on her truth. A study of the book reveals that Esther was not God's only option for liberation, but she was her family's only option.

God could have found someone else to stand up to the persecution of the Jews, but Esther's compliance with inauthenticity would negatively affect her family. In the end, Esther chose power over the illusion of peace and became a force. You're going to have to do the same. I need you to start questioning whether you've chosen an illusion of peace that requires you to stifle your authenticity.

Esther was informed that her illusion had an expiration date, and she could either wait for it to all come apart, or she could dare to beat it to the punch. God can't infuse strength into anything built on a lie. It's only in the dismantling that we are able to build our lives again with the type of structural integrity that transforms things for our entire community.

There's no better example than Esther to drive this point home because a choice she made to guard herself would have to be sacrificed if she was willing to choose establishing over protection. You can build the walls to protect yourself, or you can trust that God has placed a force field around you. Can you imagine how empowered Esther felt when she was able to maintain the life she loved and hang on to her truth at the same time? She thought it was either-or, but God placed her in a position to see that it was both-and.

Esther was the queen of Persia and a Jew. Until those truths learned to coexist, liberation for herself and her community remained out of reach. She unlocked power, changed mentalities, and learned something about herself when she broke covenant with comfort.

Now, those are the power moves I want to experience. I don't want the kind of power that comes from closing a deal, getting a man, building a business, or becoming a brand. Those things can be there one day and gone another. That kind of strength offers only fleeting enjoyment, but it does not radically change you from the inside out. There is a power that is so potent that it radically changes your life.

## LAY IT DOWN

I don't have to build walls to protect myself. God has put a force field around me.

## 14 *Limiting Beliefs*

> A woman was there who had been subject to bleeding for twelve years, but no one could heal her. She came up behind [Jesus] and touched the edge of his cloak, and immediately her bleeding stopped. "Who touched me?" Jesus asked. . . . Then the woman, seeing that she could not go unnoticed, came trembling and fell at his feet. . . . She told why she had touched him and how she had been instantly healed. Then he said to her, "Daughter, your faith has healed you. Go in peace."
>
> LUKE 8:43–45, 47–48 NIV

**IN LUKE 8 JESUS WAS ON THE HUNT BECAUSE IT WAS** important that a certain woman understand that the power she received didn't come when she reached out and grabbed His hem. After the woman realized that she could no longer stay hidden and confessed that it was she who touched His hem, Jesus said to her, "Your faith has made you well. Go in peace" (v. 48 NLT).

This was not a standard salutation but a revelation for the woman to take with her as she discovered a new life that was not restricted by the dysfunction of her old system. Jesus wanted her to know it wasn't the touch that made the difference; it was her faith. The fact that Jesus highlighted this to the woman is important because it gives us insight into how to defeat the systems in our lives that are causing us issues.

So often we wonder, *What do I need to do to stop the cycle?* Maybe instead we need to be asking, *What do I need to believe?* Or even more powerful, *What belief do I need to release?* What God wants for us is to give up the beliefs that keep us from true relationship with Him.

If you believe that you are too damaged and broken,

accomplished and successful, or average and ordinary to be treasured by God, you are wrong. God doesn't want you to just lay down the belief system that no longer serves you. But like any good altar moment, God wants to give you an exchange when you lay down your limiting belief. It is time to have a funeral for who you used to be.

God wants to reveal to you the ways His power can show up for you and through you. The cracks that make you feel fragile and powerless are the places where the power of God can take up residency and begin to dwell within you.

My goal is for you to move from a mindset of self-sabotage to system-sabotage. As you dissect your unhealthy patterns and begin to understand exactly where you continue to get stuck, the next move will be for you to resist the bad seeds. It is only through faith that the mission of breaking out is possible. Faith is not just what you believe but also who you believe.

Coming into agreement with your system of oppression is choosing to live, sleep, and partner with the enemy of your destiny. Cultivating the faith necessary to break free from what holds you back requires you to have a deeper faith that can be experienced only through relationship with God.

## LAY IT DOWN

Where my strength is weak, God's power is more than enough.

## 15 God Hunger

As the deer pants for the water brooks, so pants my soul for You, O God.

PSALM 42:1

**WHEN YOU'VE BEEN HURT BY OR ARE LEERY OF CHURCH,** it's difficult to untangle the connection between God and people. I went through this. I assumed that disappointing people was the same as disappointing God. My faith was contaminated by my interaction with people.

Just in case you're in that place, I want to share my process with you. My relationship with God started with desire. I had to admit that I desired to truly have my own intimate knowledge of God's presence in my life. My heart longed to experience the overwhelming and undeniable presence of the all-knowing, all-powerful God. You cannot be filled if you don't have hunger.

I grew up in church, and I watched and listened while many seemed to experience radical encounters. Meanwhile, I was twiddling my thumbs. I felt with certainty that something was wrong with me. I would recite the salvation prayer at the end of every sermon in hopes that even though I didn't experience what was happening in the room, at least I'd accepted Jesus into my life.

At that time, I wasn't hungry for God. I was just curious. It wasn't until my prayers reflected my desperation that I began to experience God's presence. *God, if You're still . . .* was how most of my prayers began. *If You're still listening . . . willing to give me another chance . . . good . . . here . . .* and so on, *then please reveal Yourself to me.*

It's important that we don't make a habit of buttoning up our prayers with a request for God to do things. Instead, wanting to get to know God apart from what God can do for you is the only way to truly be in relationship with Him. When you get to a place where you know God, then even when life isn't moving in the direction you anticipated, you don't charge it to God's character, because you know God too well to think He'd do anything to hurt you.

If you've fallen into thinking that God has bad intentions or no intentions for you, I want to assuage your doubts. It could not be further from the truth. Every single thing that God has created serves a purpose and adds value to creation. There's a role for you to play in this world, and only God can lead you to understand that role.

It's not enough to ask God to show up if you're not going to look for where He could be. Finding God is not as simple as waiting for a big booming voice to interrupt your day.

No, instead you have to intentionally set aside time, focus, and energy to search for God throughout your day. You'll begin to see that a stranger on the street was not just kind to you for no reason, but that God used them to reveal Himself to you. Maybe there's a message that comes your way. The person who delivered it may have a gift, but the transformation you experience is not by happenstance. That person has allowed God to work through them.

As you begin this journey of walking on water and betraying the toxic system that has become familiar, your relationship with God will be your compass. Let Him push you into the next dimension of your power.

## LAY IT DOWN

I acknowledge my soul's hunger for God and determine to search for Him throughout my day.

# 16 Grace and Self-Compassion

You live under the freedom of God's grace.
                                    ROMANS 6:14 NLT

**WHEN WE'RE JUST GOING ABOUT OUR DAYS, WE CAN** unwittingly fall into survival mode. Our goal is to simply get through the day as quickly and as unscathed as possible. When expediency becomes more important than accurately living according to our values, there will be damage.

When no intentional effort is made to ensure you're living according to the values you espouse, you will eventually find yourself drifting without an anchor. You're "eyeing" it, and you may get it right more times than you get it wrong, but there's also a chance that when you miss, you miss big.

I want you to see your core values as the measuring stick that determines if you're living up to who you are meant to be. When you compare your daily choices to the measuring stick of your values, you're able to see how you're growing.

Too often we give ourselves so much grace that we are impotent at developing the character that facilitates our power. Not that you should no longer have compassion for yourself when you miss the mark, but I want your compassion to lead to determination.

Having compassion for when you mess up is only transformational when it leads you to try again. I had to learn this in my relationship with God. I assumed His compassion was reserved for things that happened to me, not things I did to myself. Foolishly, I believed in order to receive compassion from God, I needed to be the victim, but the hard truth that no one wants to hear is how God has just as much compassion for the victim as the villain.

God understands why we make the choices we make. He knows why we are hurting, upset, disappointed, or needy. He understands why we missed the mark, but His compassion for why we missed doesn't change His desire for us to not miss again.

The commitment to relentlessly living a life aligned with your principles is how you develop integrity. When marinating on the choices you've made throughout the day and whether they aligned with your values, try to reserve judgment and excuse making. Instead, take into account the different set of values you had to rotate based on the environment and individuals in front of you. With a simple yes or no, determine if you had a value-aligned day.

It's important to understand what moves you out of the place of living in your values so that a warning flag can go up when you're experiencing those circumstances. A mindset that takes advantage of grace may say, "Oh, well. I'm human. This will probably happen again. I do well in all of these other areas, so they should be able to let me slide in this area." The problem with relying on grace is that it disguises pride. When your ego convinces you that living outside of your values is permissible, you miss out on an opportunity for humility to welcome love and compassion from the person most affected by your actions.

Compassion says, "You have been functioning without being refueled by rest and vision for so long that you can't even see yourself. You should apologize first to yourself for living outside of your values and then to those who've been affected by your inner disconnect." Then plan ways to give your mind, body, and spirit the value recalibration they long for.

## LAY IT DOWN

I will let grace overwhelm me with its faithfulness even when I am unfaithful.

# 17 Heaven Invading Earth

> We do not have a High Priest who cannot sympathize with our weaknesses, but was in all points tempted as we are, yet without sin.
>
> HEBREWS 4:15

**THERE IS SOMETHING POWERFUL ABOUT DEMONSTRAT**ing empathy when a person has noted a difference in the way they once connected with you. From that place you get to invite them into the reality of how not living up to your values, or not having values at all, was negatively affecting your confidence and relationship with God.

Not every person is trying to hold you back from growth, and some people are actually owed an explanation for why you've changed. These are people who we are walking life out with every day. They are the bonds that have been seemingly healthy as a result of you not living up to your values; therefore you may experience some discomfort as you change the way you engage.

It is my profound belief that pursuing full integration of our values is the only way we begin to foster an inner environment conducive to pursuing endeavors that require us to trust our insides.

There is a way of being that God wants to establish in you. It's not something you will suddenly wake up and have but a commitment to enacting the values of that being each day. This is a journey that even Jesus had to walk out on earth, so you will have to walk it out too. What I love about studying the life of Jesus is not just marveling at the glory of Him as a Savior but also the process He submitted to so His power could be perfected.

The Gospel of Luke tells us that though His divinity was

undeniable at birth, Jesus still had to grow in "wisdom and stature, and in favor with God and men" (Luke 2:52). Seems odd that Jesus had to grow in favor with God, who sent Him. I tend to think Jesus was just being an obedient Son, doing what His Father asked, but Jesus had a choice. He did not have to follow the path that God laid out for Him. He could have gotten to earth and chosen to modify the plan.

Instead, He embarked on a journey of being fully integrated with the human experience without losing focus on His divine mission. That's what I desire for you. I want you to experience the full integration of what it means to be human. Just like us, Jesus experienced being tired, tempted, excited, upset, focused, ambitious, and irritated, but He still clung to His values of wanting to please His Father in heaven.

Believing in Jesus is more than just being someone who attends weekly church services and knows a few scriptures. To believe in Jesus is to recognize that your life has the ability to be a gate for heaven to touch earth. Pursuing God's vision and values for our lives and living with the intention of channeling that into all we do is how heaven invades earth through us.

## LAY IT DOWN

Today, I surrender to God's purpose and plan for heaven to touch earth through me.

# 18 From Preparation to Utilization

For the joy set before [Jesus] he endured the cross, scorning its shame, and sat down at the right hand of the throne of God.
HEBREWS 12:2 NIV

**A COUPLE OF YEARS AGO I FOUND MYSELF IN NEED OF A** car. I was in the market for a full-size SUV. Finding a new car at the time was impossible, and the prices for a used car were outrageous! Much to my surprise, I found a dealership outside of the radius where we lived with a brand-new version of the car that I wanted for less than the price I was going to pay for the used version. The only caveat was the vehicle was still on the manufacturing line. I called the dealership and learned that they were expecting the car to arrive within the next few weeks. If I was willing to reserve the car and wait, it would be mine.

I've purchased a new vehicle before, but never one that came straight from the factory. I know there may not be a huge difference between it coming from the factory versus sitting on the lot for a few days or a couple of months, but in my head it was different. This car had just gotten off the factory line.

While I was thinking of all the ways I needed the additional space for my growing girls, their friends, and activities, the parts of the car were being assembled piece by piece. I was thinking of how I was going to use it; meanwhile, steel, rubber, plastic, and aluminum were being twisted and contorted to become what I would drive. Sure, alone those items have some power, but combined, they would become a machine full of force and power that commanded space on the road. Before it could become an agent of power, it had to surrender to a process that would ensure it had the structural integrity required to maintain the manufacturer's commitment to quality, comfort, and reliability.

Like the vehicle, you are well on your way to becoming an agent of power that represents heaven on earth. You started surrendering to a process long before you picked up this book, but if you've committed to doing this work, then you are moving from the realm of preparation to activation.

Soon, you'll begin to experience an alignment that can only occur when God's Word and your life are speaking the same message. You'll notice that the alignment plugs the holes where power was being drained and releases the clamp where power was being stalled. What happens next is similar to a car coming off the manufacturing line: You're going from preparation mode to utilization mode. You're going from being several parts to a vessel of power.

Many people want to be used by God, but not enough people want to be prepared by God. Jesus did not go from Mary's womb to the stranger's tomb in the same day. Over a course of time, He underwent a process that allowed His impact to be undeniable. It's not just that Jesus died on the cross for our sins. It's that Jesus became obedient to a process, even obedient to death, that required thirty years of patience in order to become our Savior.

A life spent doing the work so that we can be fit to be used by God is powerful, but our lives are not supposed to end in preparation. It would be like renovating and cleaning a home where no one is allowed to live. It's time for you to begin living in this new space.

## LAY IT DOWN

I am moving out of the undercover stage that preparation requires and getting into the action of being used to expand God's reign on the earth.

# 19 Shame's Power Broken

> Those who look to him for help will be radiant with joy; no shadow of shame will darken their faces.
>
> PSALM 34:5 NLT

**I'LL NEVER FORGET THE FIRST TIME I SHARED THE TESTI-**mony of my teen pregnancy to a room full of people. I figured once they knew, people would whisper and then scurry away from me the moment I came around. Something quite the opposite occurred instead. Women in their sixties and seventies began approaching me, their hands clasping mine as their eyes peered into my own. Then, in a hushed tone, they made me aware that I wasn't just telling my story; I was telling theirs.

For decades they'd let the power of shame silence them from sharing the fullness of their stories. They were proud of me for doing what they never felt they could. My life became evidence that the power of shame had been extracted from holding a teen mother down and was now being used to set another teen mom free.

When I think about the many exchanges I've had with older women who share similar scars, I wonder whether the times changed naturally or if by telling my truth I somehow forced time to adjust. In other words, are we waiting for our scars to lose influence over us, or are we allowing the scars to hold more power than they deserve?

What if those women who were in their seventies would've decided twenty or even thirty years prior that they were going to dare to embrace God's grace and be made whole? I ponder this because I don't want you to miss the moment when what you once thought held power no longer does.

Becoming a force is when your confidence gives you the

courage to be a solution to what's happening around you. If we make confidence about how we fit in our clothes or how we want others to perceive us, we will miss the moment when confidence has the ability to make us a force that doesn't need validation from possessing a certain image.

There is a confidence that awakens you to the truth that the things you once thought had the power to keep you from doing something for God have now become a pebble you kick to the side so you can finally move with a divine stride.

Jesus knew that the miracles He was performing did not require a certain environment. He traveled all throughout His land preaching the gospel and performing miracles. Jesus trusted that He worked wherever God sent Him. It would be nice if we could stay in the same city with our same people for as long as possible, but sometimes destiny requires that we move to foreign places.

Sometimes we confuse familiarity with confidence and don't want to change because we're afraid that we'll fail. God did not call you to success without scars. God has called you to the sacred journey of trusting Him through failure and disappointment. Maybe you should stop asking yourself if you can change and still be great and instead begin asking if you can stay the same and still experience God's new mercy.

## LAY IT DOWN

I have access to the type of confidence that pushes me in the direction of what I once thought was impossible.

# 20 The Jagged Edges

> The purposes of a person's heart are deep waters, but one who has insight draws them out.
>
> PROVERBS 20:5 NIV

**I WANT TO UNPACK WITH YOU THE WAYS YOU GO FROM** being merely an individual who feels inconsequential to becoming a force that cannot be denied. Our function on the earth is not to be just viewers but to actively engage in such a way that the earth looks different as a result of our presence. It's hard to get to this stage when we're consumed with the work of being delivered from our fears and insecurities, but once you get a taste of partnering with God to make the world better, you can never forget that level of fulfillment.

The partnership takes courage, and sometimes it does feel like you're taking a risk, but what's happening inside you must come out so that the world can experience light where there was once darkness.

No doubt the world is not short on problems these days. We can allow this to discourage us, or we can see it as a clarion call to engage.

This is a much larger prayer than "God, give me the power to lose weight, get rich, or find a partner." I believe that God wants for your life to be happy and your soul to thrive, but part of being in any good relationship is asking the other person what we can do for them. When we think this way, we may realize that God wants to use the jagged edges of our past to help someone nurse their own wounds.

It's so important that you make your growth about you for a season so that when the time is right, you can spend a lifetime serving those who need your wisdom the most. When you perform an autopsy on what has died and come back to life inside yourself, you're better able to guide others through, or away from, the pitfalls that had you bound.

This is about you becoming an active participant in the change you want to see happen in the world. Jesus could have ascended to heaven after being raised from the dead and said His work was complete, but He visited the disciples because they'd been exposed to too much power to stay where He'd left them. He gave them a charge to spread the power they'd received.

Is there a problem you are constantly seeing? Have you asked God what role you can play in the solution? Are you waiting on someone to fix something that you're bothered by, or are you willing to risk discomfort to be the solution?

Imagine a house that has been renovated but not lived in. It has undergone a process but has not been put to use. On one hand, that's great because the house stays in picture-perfect working condition. To live in the house, you will risk things breaking, burning out, being stained, and being damaged. You cannot avoid the potential power failures that come with being a solution, but with each failure comes an even more powerful realization. Each failure carries with it a lesson that can recharge you for your next attempt.

## LAY IT DOWN

I open my heart to the possibility that my gifts could be what God wants to use to bring order and restoration where things are in disarray.

## 21 Living a Fruitful Life

> The Lord God took the man and put him in the garden of Eden to tend and keep it.
>
> GENESIS 2:15

**WHENEVER I HEAR THE CREATION STORY, I ALWAYS THINK** that when God presented the earth to Adam, He gave him a finished product. The immediate idea that comes to mind features two people in a perfectly climate-controlled garden where they could easily pick their breakfast from a tree, take a nap, pet some animals, dip in the river, and sunbathe.

Even when we talk about presently suffering through the consequences of their mistake in the garden, we talk about it like Adam and Eve interrupted what would have been a life akin to vacationing and forced us to clock into a life full of labor and hard work.

No doubt their mistake intensified the physical, emotional, and spiritual labor connected to our existence, but when I look at Genesis 1:28, what I see is the reality that God always intended for us to spend portions of our lives pursuing productivity. When God gave them dominion over the earth, the earth itself was just a seed. They were charged with the responsibility of bringing it to its full potential.

The first thing that God told Adam and Eve after He said to be fruitful and multiply was to fill the earth. Most theologians agree that being fruitful and multiplying is the act of having a family. I believe this is in part what God meant, but I don't think it was limited to having children for the sake of having children. I believe that God ultimately desired for them to be intentional about multiplying His image on earth. As we know, that's not just having sex and creating children. That's truly living a life that models what receiving God's love, affirmation, validation, and purpose can look like. It's living a life that is worthy of impartation.

God's original intention was for the earth to take on the attributes of heaven. He gave Adam and Eve a formula for how to make that happen, but sin's entrance built a wall that made the earth a mixture of heaven, hell, humanity, fear, decadence, and pain. Now, if I were God, I would've gone about minding my business, but He did not let go of the notion that heaven could still find a home on earth. He just realized we were going to need some support to get it done.

Jesus came to restore the bridge between heaven and earth. When Jesus professed that the kingdom of heaven was at hand, He was letting us know there is no more division between heaven and earth. Had Adam and Eve not been disobedient in the garden, the kingdom of heaven would have been established through them, fulfilling the original mandate given to them in Genesis.

Even if children are not in the plan for your life, it doesn't mean you can't be fruitful. You are able to become fruitful by taking the seeds God has placed in you and bringing them to fruition. You multiply when you make sure the fruit of your life doesn't end with you.

## LAY IT DOWN

I am not just a person taking up space on this planet. I am a seed-thrower.

## 22  A Solid Base

Be fruitful and multiply.

GENESIS 1:22 NLT

**IN GENESIS 1, GOD TOLD HIS FRESH CREATION THAT THEY** needed to fill the earth. Now, either God really wanted the earth to be full of people so He mentioned it three different times—be fruitful, multiply, and fill the earth—or God was not referring exclusively to procreation. God was giving them an insight that only He fully understood.

As lush and as full as their surroundings may have been, they were only a portion of what's possible in the earth. The garden of Eden was not the only place on earth. It's just the place that God created to be their home. Genesis 2:8–9 lets us know that the environment God placed them in was to be a place that was beautiful and delicious: "The LORD God planted a garden eastward in Eden, and there He put the man whom He had formed. And out of the ground the LORD God made every tree grow that is pleasant to the sight and good for food. The tree of life was also in the midst of the garden, and the tree of the knowledge of good and evil."

Later on in verse 15 it says, "Then the LORD God took the man and put him in the garden of Eden to tend and keep it."

Why would God give them the responsibility of subduing the earth and having dominion over the fish of the sea, the birds of the air, and every living thing that moves on the earth, then relegate them to staying and tending to a flourishing garden? God knew their existence would extend beyond their initial territory.

Whether by exploration or exile, they would see that the place where they started would not be the place where they landed. I love when a scripture gives us insight into the character of God. Here I learn that you need a solid base before you can reasonably expand.

Far too many people beat themselves up for not being further along in life, but they fail to take into consideration how far they've come considering the instability in their base. If you've gone from sinking foundation to sinking foundation, it can frustrate you and make you believe you're incapable of establishing.

When Adam and Eve were banished from the garden, they lost life as they'd known it. However, they didn't lose the fundamental base that even when God holds you accountable, He doesn't forsake you or abandon you. That's the only kind of base worth building on over and over.

In my head I imagine that Adam and Eve walked out of the garden, and it was like two people from a ritzy private school being dropped off to record an episode of *Scared Straight*. It immediately became clear that what Adam and Eve were exposed to in the garden was a stark contrast to the reality they were experiencing outside the garden.

They must have had an aha moment when they realized that life outside the garden, though full of creatures and habitats, was also empty. What they'd been exposed to helped them understand the possibilities of what could happen in the uncultivated land where they were banished. Sometimes what you have been exposed to won't make sense until you get to where God is taking you.

## LAY IT DOWN

I am in the process of establishing a firm foundation so I can build without fear of irreparable demolition.

## 23 Fill an Empty Place

Fill the earth and subdue it.

GENESIS 1:28 NIV

**SOMETIMES I FIND MYSELF LOGGING OFF SOCIAL MEDIA** just to clear my head because the world is full of so many voices. I turn on the TV to watch something entertaining, and even though there's plenty to watch, everything still looks empty.

I drive through my city and see how quickly things are developing and wonder what will be taking up space where there is vacancy in the next five to ten years. I am constantly having to remind myself that just because the world looks full doesn't mean it's not empty.

I am convinced that when God looks at our world, He's not distracted by the standing structures. God sees the busy souls that are still empty. God sees the bustling cities that are still empty. God sees the full churches with leaders who are still empty.

So how do we fill the earth? We add the substance of our inspired growth and development in bearing God's image into the conversation. It may seem unnecessary to add more noise into an already busy world, but God's given a unique offering that will break through the noise and fill in the emptiness of the person who needs your voice the most.

You can break through the clamoring of your family's culture and your friends' norms. You don't have to wait until you're polished and eloquent before raising your voice in opposition to what has become acceptable. Breaking through the noise begins with occupying the territory where fear, anger, bitterness, ego, and pride have left holes in the confidence and power of your community.

You'd be surprised how much distinction you carry when your gifts and talents are not an imitation of what someone else has said or done. The authentic release of you has undeniable power that can fill the earth. It doesn't matter how many people are doing the thing you do. If God has laid it on your heart to do, it's so that you can fill an empty spot.

Part of being a solution is searching for the place where you've experienced God's faithfulness and allowing your life to serve as a testimony. Think about the ways you have become full and how you could pour into someone else.

Too often we say we want to break a generational curse, but we're not truly focused on the curse. We're focused on the outcome of the curse. You want to end teen pregnancy, financial insecurity, toxic communication patterns, and unhealthy relationship dynamics. Those are systems that exist in your family, but the power to break those systems happens when you become a force that moves differently.

When you trust that God has anointed your next shift to have enough power to not just move you but everything connected to you, then you will become a force.

Like a kite waiting on a gust of wind, I feel in my spirit that someone reading this needs to know that your community is waiting on you to change their path. You may not even be the most qualified in your family to do it. Don't allow your position to make you believe you don't have what it takes to bring under control what has been wreaking havoc on your family and community.

## LAY IT DOWN

I no longer have to pretend that I'm not who I am. I add value where there was emptiness.

## 24 Present and Engaged

We have this treasure in jars of clay to show that this all-surpassing power is from God and not from us.

2 CORINTHIANS 4:7 NIV

**WHEN PEOPLE BEGAN ATTACHING THE TERM** *POWERHOUSE* to my name and messages, I began to question the accessibility and definition of *power*. I needed to research *power* because there was nothing in me that felt powerful. I think that's because I thought being powerful should feel a certain way. I thought it would ease insecurities and release me from nerves and anxiety.

Turns out being powerful doesn't mean you'll feel like a big-shot boss who takes no prisoners. You'll still have to wrestle with all the emotions that make us question ourselves. Being powerful means you give yourself permission to live authentically, to be honest about your capabilities, desires, needs, and feelings.

Recently, I asked my social media audience when they feel the most powerful. Most of them answered with particular moments that fill their tanks. The answers ranged from getting their hair done to completing tasks, finishing big projects, first waking up in the morning, and oddly enough, cracking their toes. I definitely didn't dig in to that one.

Almost 90 percent of the answers came down to fleeting moments. I could relate. When people started calling me a powerhouse, I wanted to study what was happening to me in the moment I was speaking because I wanted it to translate into everything that I did. I went to my therapist to figure out how I can take what's happening in the moment of a message and make it show up when I'm going about my everyday life.

When I'm completely tapped in to the zone required for me

to deliver a message, I'm not self-conscious about anything. I trust fully what God has given me, and I step out of my reserved nature to do whatever it takes for the word God's given me to become flesh. The force and power on display when I was preaching was something I longed to experience in my everyday rhythm. It wasn't long before I realized that part of the reason I felt a disconnect between the moments when I was speaking and the moments when I was just going about my everyday life is because I thought power could have only one expression.

Perhaps that's the reason most of the people in my social media audience experienced fleeting moments of power too. Maybe we need to release our limited perspective on what power is and how it's expressed. Then we might experience the steady flow of power that is ever present.

When we practice being wholly aware, we're able to accurately gauge and assess how to respond and connect with whoever or whatever is in front of us. We must be willing to ask ourselves, *What does my being powerful in this particular context look like?*

## LAY IT DOWN

I am my most powerful when I am fully present and engaged in what is happening before me.

# 25 Power at Rest

The LORD is my shepherd. . . . He lets me rest in green meadows; he leads me beside peaceful streams. He renews my strength.

PSALM 23:1-3 NLT

**WHEN I FIRST BEGAN WORKING OUT WITH A PERSONAL** trainer, I found myself getting winded and feeling exerted in the first set. I chalked it up to being out of shape. My endurance began to increase, but I felt I couldn't fully feel the advantage of my muscles getting stronger because the trainer would consistently increase the weight.

Mentally, I knew I was getting stronger because I was lifting heavier weights than when I started, but I couldn't feel the additional strength in my body. Because he would increase the weight before I could experience the gratification of knowing I'd gotten stronger, I never got a chance to not feel tired so quickly.

One day I finally asked him why he wouldn't let me just keep lifting the lighter weight for a week, so I wasn't always feeling like I was starting from scratch. He let me know that our training sessions were not going to be the place where my ego could be fed about how much stronger I was getting. It's what I did outside of our sessions that would reveal just how much power I was gaining. He emphasized that as long as I was resting and stretching, I would see how my body was transforming. If I didn't feel powerful in my training sessions, I'd have to commit to a routine of resting and stretching that allowed me to see the power I was building to show up in my day-to-day responsibilities.

It dawned on me that the work I was putting in at the gym could not translate into power unless I took the time to stretch, rest, and recover. Isn't it crazy how the thing we think should grant us power doesn't? It's actually the thing that doesn't seem like it matters at all that produces our power. For strength training, it is the resting and stretching.

God did not stop being all-powerful on the seventh day when He decided to rest. He just understood what would make Him most powerful for that day was not creating but resting. I want to talk about this because I've seen too many fall into the trap of believing that they are only as powerful as their output, but not their input.

There's no use in us talking about you becoming a force if you think the only way you can become a force is by pushing through even when you're hurting, depressed, sad, and overwhelmed. The nature of being a force requires that we truly respect the other forces at play in our lives. You are not an island. Try as hard as you like, but you still will not be able to avoid that you must engage in a whirlwind world and dare to keep your head in the game.

I don't want you to strain yourself trying to exert your power over the forces that are working against your development. There will be moments when you may have to let the other forces win a round so that you can maintain your peace.

## LAY IT DOWN

The times when I don't feel like I'm doing anything powerful may be the moments I'm growing the most.

## 26 Space for Recovery

> David inquired of the Lord, "Shall I go and attack the Philistines? Will you deliver them into my hands?"
>
> 2 SAMUEL 5:19 NIV

**WHEN THERE IS NO WIND IN YOUR SAILS AND YOU FEEL** you are all out of ability, that's when you will discover that the most powerful thing you can do is not lift heavier weights and for longer periods of time, but rest your decision-making muscles and stretch your faith. The power of recovery keeps us from making decisions dictated by the pressure of negative forces. It helps us remember our ultimate goal of alignment with God.

Learning to decipher between when you should be going harder and when you fall back is not easy, but I believe they both have the same starting point. In our relationship with God, we're able to admit that we are in over our heads. In the safety of His counsel, we're able to say we are overwhelmed by our sea of responsibilities.

The Old Testament depicts several encounters that David had with his adversaries. Each time, before he'd face off to engage with them in battle, he'd ask God, "Shall I go up?" He asked this question at times when he was still licking his wounds from the other battle. He brought it up in moments when he was unsure whether he'd have support from his army.

The same David that trusted a stone and slingshot wanted to make sure he didn't push through at the expense of being outside of God's covering and support. David understood that his enemies were a respectable opponent and a force in their own right, but so was his God. He didn't want to pursue anything that didn't have God's blessing on it.

A few of us mess up because we ask God whether a certain battle is ours to fight; we've already put on our armor, gathered the troops, and headed into battle. It's difficult to get a clear answer from God when we're fully invested in the outcome we prefer. A true answer from God about the best expenditure of your power can be realized only from a place of total divestment. I shouldn't have to tell you this because you know better than I do, but we make the worst decisions when we're tired or emotionally and spiritually blinded.

When sizing up all that you're up against, the best decision you can make is no decision at all. Turn all of the energy you're exerting into making a decision and channel it into forcing yourself into a space of rest. Anxiety has been known to push us all to make a decision that promises to end our misery, but more often than not, the decision compounds our misery instead of ending it. Rest is better than regret.

A person who is moving with power cannot adequately devise a plan to overthrow their adversary from a place of fear. It means you're allowing fear to move you and not faith. Gone are the days of making a rash decision about your finances, relationships, career, meals, or trips. Instead, consider asking yourself what's driving you to make a decision right now.

You can trust what's driving your choices only when you are able to rest in the reality that God's going to take care of you.

## LAY IT DOWN

I can rest in the knowledge that whatever I'm facing can only teach me and not break me.

## 27 Room for Restoration

No weapon formed against you shall prosper.

ISAIAH 54:17

**ISN'T IT INTERESTING THAT IN GENESIS 3, WHEN THE** serpent wanted to thwart Adam and Eve from having dominion, he did not make them question themselves?

He made them question God—and indirectly themselves.

Could they trust they were made in the image of God? Could they trust the authority and dominion God gave them? Those questions changed the way they saw everything. If someone threw a can of paint on your mirror, you might find a little corner that is unaffected. But eventually the strain of trying to see through the paint would make you weary. You'd stop looking in the mirror altogether.

If you no longer see God with clear eyes, you can't see your potential. Jesus came to clean the mirror that keeps you from seeing God and, ultimately, yourself properly. Through His model He demonstrates to us what it means to be a human made in the image of God.

When you realize your path is clear, the Enemy must work even harder to keep you from turning and allowing the life of Jesus to transform the way you view your life. You'll notice that the moment you begin to walk in truth and wisdom, it feels like all kinds of distractions are in your way.

You're not going crazy; the force is real. It is trying to keep you from true relationship with Jesus and from having a heart posture that receives a perfect love that casts out fear. When you begin to feel the resistance and strain from this opposition, you have an opportunity to introduce a greater force that isn't rooted in physical strength but rather in spiritual development.

Prayer and worship are the most powerful forces we have against the demonic forces scheming to stunt our growth.

When we experience resistance, it can be hard to determine whether we should lean into God's presence or create a practical strategy. When you're used to having to figure things out on your own, it creates a rhythm of making a game plan to overcome whatever obstacle is in your way before spending time in prayer or worship. Then there comes a time when dancing to the beat of your own drum wears you down.

Instead of becoming overwhelmed by our lack of ability to push toward our desire, we have to go back to the drawing board to make sure what we're trying to accomplish has been graced to overcome resistance. How do you do this? The answer is one you won't want to hear, but here it is anyway: Do nothing.

If we can trust that rest is not resignation, we can give our most precious resources the time they need to recover and come back stronger, while also giving God the room to restore a vision for our lives that does not center on forcing things to happen but on us becoming a force released into the earth.

Resisting the temptation to be the captain of our own ship will require focus, dedication, and trust in God above all. From the place of rest, you may recognize where you got off-center. You may realize that when you started pursuing a goal or creating a project, you were full of faith and power, but the fear of it not happening created desperation.

It is possible that you may need to reclaim your identity from the desired results of a situation.

## LAY IT DOWN

Before I determine what natural steps I may need to take, through prayer and worship I exercise authority over evil.

## 28  A Force Among Forces

Then Jesus was led up by the Spirit into the wilderness to be tempted by the devil.

MATTHEW 4:1

**IN MY EXPERIENCE THERE ARE TWO TYPES OF PEOPLE IN** the world. One type of person dreams so often that sometimes going to sleep gives them anxiety. They're afraid that when they close their eyes, a wild ride into their imagination, fears, dreams, and even prolific messages from God await them.

I am not one of those people. If the good Lord doesn't tell me before I drift off to sleep, He's going to have to wait until the alarm or my spirit wakes me up. This doesn't mean that when I'm awake I don't go on wild rides, nor do I escape wrestling with my fears and dreams.

No matter what, we all must face the reality of what it means to be human. You being human doesn't make you any less of a force. It just means that preserving the power that makes you a force requires you to have a focus more powerful than your detractors.

Detractors are agents of your opposition meant to detract your power and render you incapable of clinging to the faith, power, and focus required for your mission. There are no better examples of a detractor on a mission than the Serpent in the garden of Eden (Genesis 3) and the tempter in the wilderness (Matthew 4). Both of these scenarios, though separated substantially by generations, represent a full-circle moment available to us all.

In these two texts we have a woman who did not know she was a force among forces juxtaposed with Jesus, who was born with the knowledge that He was a force among forces. Going back to Genesis 1:28, God did not make it known that Adam and Eve should beware of forces that may detract them from fulfilling the mission He'd given them. Why didn't the all-knowing, all-powerful God tell them what to look out for? I know my thoughts are not His thoughts and my ways are not His ways (Isaiah 55:8), but I know from raising children that even when I warn them about something in advance, they don't always take seriously the threat that is before them. There are moments when firsthand experience from less-than-ideal choices grabs your attention more quickly than a warning from God.

Jesus, born into Judaism, would've had full knowledge of the original sin in the garden, as well as His parents' knowledge that His birth would be contested by many. Jesus' life before the moment in the garden of Gethsemane was likely steeped with the awareness that active forces were at play, desiring to see His ministry end before it fully began.

His first confrontation with such a force came in the wilderness when the tempter visited Him. In analyzing the approach that the Serpent took in Genesis versus Matthew, I noticed a pattern worthy of sharing with you. This pattern is essential for you to understand because it will aid you in recognizing the tactics that forces of darkness may wield against you.

In neither account did Jesus or the woman volunteer to show off the power they possessed. This perspective is important because too often we fall into the trap of trying to prove the power we possess by actively searching for an opponent. God is giving you power to go and grow, not to conquer and boast.

## LAY IT DOWN

I have nothing to prove. Growth happens as I respond to God.

## 29 Holy Rhythm

> I have come down from heaven to do the will of God who sent me, not to do my own will.
>
> JOHN 6:38 NLT

**HOW MANY THINGS DO YOU DO IN YOUR LIFE FROM A PLACE** of wanting to be acknowledged and validated? When I'm running on fumes, I want cheerleaders to come out and celebrate that I brushed my teeth in the morning.

Then there are moments when I receive a testimony from someone who expresses that my ministry changed their life. They thank me for saying yes to God's will for my life, and I make sure to let them know that the honor is truly mine because I know without a shadow of a doubt that what they're experiencing is not me at all. If they never said thank you and I never got a testimony, I'd still be sharing what God gives me in some capacity, because what I want to hear above anything else is, "Well done, good and faithful servant" (Matthew 25:21).

You will never be distracted from your mission by what you already have. The attack against your destiny will always center around what you think you lack.

One of the things that made faith challenging for me growing up is that it seemed like everything Jesus accomplished on earth was done with ease. I think we can spend so much time focused on the divinity of Jesus that we miss the opportunity to truly acknowledge His full humanity. When we consider Jesus as a human being similar to ourselves, we'll see that His laying down His life was not something done easily or cavalierly.

Jesus was not an indestructible superhero who went running into burning buildings. Jesus was thoughtful about what actions

He would take and when. Jesus' fame grew, but not because He wanted to make His name great.

In the wilderness the devil tempted Jesus:

> "If you are the Son of God . . . throw yourself down. For it is written: 'He will command his angels concerning you, and they will lift you up in their hands, so that you will not strike your foot against a stone.'"
>
> Jesus answered him, "It is also written: 'Do not put the Lord your God to the test.'"
>
> Again, the devil took him to a very high mountain and showed him all the kingdoms of the world and their splendor. "All this I will give you," he said, "if you will bow down and worship me."
>
> Jesus said to him, "Away from me, Satan! For it is written: 'Worship the Lord your God, and serve him only.'" (Matthew 4:6–10 NIV)

The power of the temptation was real, and it was so heavy that it required forty days and forty nights of fasting and praying. There are going to be moments when the only way you can overcome the forces attempting to derail you is if you insist on a rhythm of connection with God that models what Jesus displayed in the garden.

## LAY IT DOWN

I gain the strength to withstand temptation as I connect with God and recognize what He has already given me.

## 30 Controlling the Self

"Get out of here, Satan," Jesus told him. "For the Scriptures say . . ."

MATTHEW 4:10 NLT

**JESUS RECOGNIZED THAT WHILE HE MIGHT NOT BE ABLE** to control what other forces attempted to throw His way, He could refuse the temptation to abuse His power by putting Satan in his place. Had Jesus given in to temptation, He would have allowed the power God granted Him to be used to advance the plan of the Enemy. Jesus was the only One who could grant Satan access to His power. He didn't just ignore the attacks and wait for them to go away. He fought back by reminding Himself why He could not follow through with the suggestions of the tempter.

Too often we fight back in an effort to control our Enemy, when in reality the only person we can control is ourselves. If you're going to be a person of honor and integrity, your journey will not go uncontested. Many will seek to detract you with temptations or distractions. You can ask them to no longer show up in a capacity that hinders you, or you can put parameters on your relationship for what you will or will not allow.

You know what I love about how Jesus responded to the tempter? He didn't pretend He wasn't hungry. He didn't immediately tell the tempter to leave Him alone. In an effort to seem unfazed, we often lie to cover our weakness instead of redirecting our thoughts toward where our focus should really lie. When temptation gets real, don't pretend it has no power. Instead, introduce what has more power.

You may have to audibly remind yourself that financial stability is more powerful than the purchase you're considering.

Don't just battle temptation in your head. Use your words to push temptation back. Declaring with a whisper even when you can't say it with a yell is enough to serve notice to hell.

Jesus answered the Serpent with the words from His disciplined spirit that would not just edify Himself but also reveal His mindset to the tempter. Instead of talking back to the Enemy, allow your spirit to tell your mind what it needs to hear.

Your mind may start to betray you and make you believe you do not have the ability to move in power on earth. You may have a history of defeat that has become a weapon against your destiny, but God can use the words that come out of your mouth to push your enemy back. I'm not just talking about the spiritual forces we cannot see.

When you're tempted to be distracted by gossip, choosing to say instead, "I no longer want to be someone who finds pleasure in tearing someone down," is not just a declaration to your audience. It's your spirit reminding your mind who you are becoming.

In each of Jesus' points of engagement with the tempter, He recited what had been written in the sacred book of Judaism. If you are coming to a place in your journey where the confrontation with other forces is beginning to render you speechless because you don't have the language or knowledge of Scripture to speak that which can edify you, I want you to dive into a Bible. The same words that healed, restored, and delivered then have the power to do so now.

## LAY IT DOWN

When I don't have the strength to put the Enemy in his place, the least I can do is refuse to allow him to pull me out of my position.

## 31  Beyond Envy

> I have learned the secret of being content in any and every situation, whether well fed or hungry, whether living in plenty or in want.
>
> PHILIPPIANS 4:12 NIV

**AS HUMANS WE HAVE A BAD HABIT OF ESTEEMING A PERSON** with such high regard that we fail to see that they're human. We become so mesmerized by their talent or gift that they become larger-than-life icons. It doesn't matter how many times we hear that someone is just like us, we still find ourselves in shock when evidence emerges that reveals they're normal.

For the individual on the receiving end of such an iconic perception, maintaining a sense of identity outside of what they do, as well as mental and emotional wellness, is imperative. If not, they find themselves suffering when new voices and talents emerge, and the spotlight begins to shift to someone else.

The spotlight shifting is not limited to prominent figures. We experience this in our social circles as well. The spotlight shifts to a close friend while you're still recovering from a loss. Or you're marveling at your latest victory while your sibling is nursing defeat. There is probably no better example of the way the power of attention, acknowledgment, and celebration moves than in how it shows up in our relationships.

Have you ever seen a movie where you're trying to figure out who the main star is? The opening scene seemingly follows one person until they collide into another person, and then you realize that the first character was just a bridge to the main star. Life can very much feel this way. It's as if we're participating in a series of recurring opening scenes where we fluctuate from being the main star to a supporting cast member. I've had many people come up to me and state that they're anxiously waiting for the time when it's "their season." I interpret this to mean that the person is waiting for the moment when they consistently feel like the main character who is experiencing victory and triumph instead of struggling in the background of someone else's story.

Then there are other people who've been the main character for so long that they'd like a break. Sometimes we like to call these people "the strong friend." They show up for people so frequently that they've unknowingly become the main character in most people's stories, but we never get to truly understand their desires, needs, pains, and joys.

We cannot reasonably discuss what it means to be a force who experiences outside interference without taking the time to also acknowledge that there's no such thing as a singular force. You are a force among forces. Some of those forces are intent on destruction and detracting you from purpose. Other forces are clumsily navigating this thing called life and bumping into you along the way. You must give space for the people in your life to stand tall while you're falling back.

That statement is easy to write but more challenging to implement. I love an individual with relentless determination and commitment to growth, but I also realize no one is an island, and everyone is navigating their own share of ups and downs. It won't always be your time to shine, and when you are able to move beyond envy to gratitude, you'll notice that it changes everything.

## LAY IT DOWN

Whether it's my time to shine or to pull back and rest, I know God is orchestrating every event of my life.

## 32 False Confidence

Let each of you look out not only for his own interests, but also for the interests of others.

PHILIPPIANS 2:4

**CONSIDER HOW YOU CAN ENGAGE IN A LIFESTYLE THAT** trusts when your power is dormant, someone else's can be active in a way that preserves you and prepares them. You were not meant to burn with power every single second of your life. Not even your phone can handle constantly being powered on. Trusting the other forces in your life is one way of being able to experience the much-needed shutdown that every powerful person needs.

I'd like to challenge you to not just think about quick vacations. Too often we think about taking breaks as if we're going to hit Pause on our lives and then jump right back in with the same cast, plot, and pace as before.

Making room for people to show up in their power, even when it's different from your own, is an exercise in releasing control that can strain a muscle. Luckily, the muscle that suffers when this occurs is pride, and more often than not, it needs to be strained.

I've often wondered what the difference is between being confident and being prideful. Having unearthed many insecurities, I've found myself pursuing accomplishments that can act as a balm for the areas where I've been wounded. I've thought that even though I may not have excelled in one area, at least I'll have a trophy from another area to make up the difference.

I was wrong. I thought that piling accomplishments over insecurities was like putting concealer over a blemish, but I lived in fear that the concealer would not be enough in certain environments. So I sought to achieve more and more. When you build a life accumulating things that make you proud of who you are, you never experience true confidence.

False confidence is when you're only as confident as your titles and accomplishments. Subtly, we see pride showing up in our insistence to do things our way. Pride shows up in how we look down on others for the choices and decisions they've made. It's stealthy when it seeps in and is difficult to arrest, but pride blinds us from being compassionate with ourselves and others.

It's important for us to distinguish between confidence and pride because pride is rooted in how much bigger or better you can become than others and, surprisingly, how much bigger and better you can be compared to who you once were. I'm sure you've heard or read someone say that the only person they want to be better than is the person they were yesterday. I've probably said it myself.

On the surface this seems empowering and humble, but it doesn't lay a foundation of true confidence. If the only way you can become better is to see who you were yesterday as inadequate, your confidence is constantly being demolished.

Being better than you were yesterday may not be possible. Your yesterday can be peak adulting behavior filled with timeliness, patience, and discipline. Tomorrow you could regress to who you were five years ago with one phone call. On those days, if you lay your head down in shame, you know what you're pursuing is not actually confidence but pride.

Finding a way to love every step of your journey while still moving toward progress is the only way to arrest pride.

## LAY IT DOWN

I release my grip on perfectionism and choose to be patient with myself and others.

## 33 We Are Not Islands

Two are better than one, because they have a good reward for their labor. For if they fall, one will lift up his companion.

ECCLESIASTES 4:9–10

**ONE OF MY TEACHERS, ESTHER PEREL, SHARED WITH ME** a quote about esteem that has stuck with me. "Self-esteem is seeing yourself as a flawed person, and still holding yourself in high regard." If you're able to hold yourself in high regard only when you are blind to your flaws, pride has become the architect of your life.

Arresting pride requires intentionally putting yourself in situations where you disengage from things you know you're great at and support someone else's attempt at mastery. Your role is not to conform them to your way but to give them the space to discover what works best for them.

You could even take it a step further and ask how you can support their method. There are few things more humbling than becoming a servant to a vision that is not your own. When you connect with someone and have the heart to serve their vision, you posture yourself to become a student to different methods of accomplishing tasks.

I've had to grapple with pride in every area of my life, from parenting to team building. There's a certain way I believe the household should be run. It checks all the boxes that are important to me, and I often run myself ragged trying to get it done. When I enlist my husband to help, I try to bite my tongue while he navigates the morning routine his way.

When I finally stopped measuring his effort against my expectation, I was able to learn the ways he does things differently than I do. Okay, I'll be honest. Some things aren't just different—they're actually better.

Pride is arrested when we embrace that because our lives are interconnected, everything we do is larger than just one life. We should make space for the reality that myopic thinking is the easiest way to sever ties with others and become an island.

When we are consumed with our workload, it can be challenging to recognize that we're not pushing the ball forward alone. Nothing happens in our lives that is not affected by someone else's choice. Whether we admit it or not, we are experiencing our societies, projects, and responsibilities as a collective.

This truth means there is a possibility that someone's plate is just as full as mine, yet they're finding a way forward too. It also means that nine times out of ten, my plate is lighter because of a load someone else is carrying. Ignoring the collective makes it more difficult for us to honor and value the people in our world who are giving us momentum.

It's easy to see how negative behaviors have an adverse effect. But how often do we intentionally celebrate how the combined ingenuity of a few can create exponential impact on many?

The power of the collective shifts even the most challenging atmosphere. It is impossible to do anything on earth without partnership. Even God partnered with a woman to bring salvation. Navigating the complexities of life will require strategic alliances and partnerships. When those partnerships share the same goal, nothing can stand in their way.

## LAY IT DOWN

I am not alone. I do not need to carry my burdens alone. God has put people in my life with whom to partner.

## 34 Joining Forces

> One day . . . Jesus went up on a mountain to pray, and he prayed to God all night. At daybreak he called together all of his disciples and chose twelve of them to be apostles.
>
> LUKE 6:12–13 NLT

**I LOVE HGTV. I AM ALWAYS CAPTIVATED BY HOW A** designer can take empty spaces and make them practical and beautiful. What's even more meaningful is seeing the homeowner come back into their newly renovated home with gratitude because someone was able to transfer what was important to them into their personal space.

The interior designer understands that success is not about just filling the space with trinkets and things, but filling the space based on the values of the individual they are serving in the moment. The process can be tedious and may require patience, but being unrelenting in making sure the person's desires show up in the home is worth the wait.

I use this as an example of how we navigate relationships with others. Connection must be more than filling a void of friendship, companionship, or productivity. Shared values ensure that relationships are not just placeholders but mutually edifying and beneficial. When a person does not seek to understand our values and begins to overdeliver in areas that don't matter, while underdelivering in the spaces we care about the most, we get frustrated.

If you're going to join forces with someone, you have to trust that you and the person have explored where you share values. You must believe that the partnership will not thwart your growth and development. While there are countless examples of strategic partnerships in Scripture, I am not sure one speaks to the power of joining forces better than Jesus and His disciples. Jesus did not start His ministry without first taking the time to make sure He would not have to go at it alone.

Sure, there were moments when no one could fulfill the task but Him, like when He was on the cross. However, the moments we see Jesus alone in ministry are rare compared to the moments when He had His trusted three disciples with Him. Jesus recognized that the backgrounds of His disciples would be instrumental in realizing the larger-than-life mission ahead of Him.

He did not choose the first twelve people who signed up. Nor did he put them to work immediately. Jesus journeyed with the disciples first. I believe that part of His inviting the disciples to follow Him was due to His wanting to get to know them before granting them access and bestowing them with power.

Before even giving them a task, Jesus granted them the power of access. Imagine how differently we would handle our hearts if we realized it's not just about what someone does with their access that is powerful, but the access itself is power. When you give someone access to your heart, dreams, thoughts, and fears, you are beginning the process of joining forces with them.

You don't have to jump the gun on filling the void just because you think you may have prospective material in an opportunity or candidate. Taking the time to understand a person's values and how they align with your own can ensure that when you join forces, you become stronger. There's nothing that God is going to do on earth that will not require you to join forces, because everything that will be accomplished is too large for one life.

## LAY IT DOWN

I will be open to joining forces with people God brings into my life.

## 35 No Need to Isolate

As iron sharpens iron, so one person sharpens another.
PROVERBS 27:17 NIV

**BECOMING VULNERABLE TO PEOPLE IS NOT MY FAVORITE** hobby, but I'd be lying if I said I haven't reaped the rewards of falling back so someone else can come forth. In the process of doing that, I've been able to increase and expand the vision God's given me for my life, family, gifts, talents, and influence in a way that would not have been possible without joining forces.

Even my books are an example of what happens when a message is amplified through the support of others. I wonder what could be amplified in your life by you joining forces. Could your peace be amplified by joining forces with someone else who shares your values?

There's a story in the Bible about two women named Mary and Elizabeth. Both experienced miraculous pregnancies. When Mary learned she was going to conceive even though she'd never been with a man, the angel Gabriel told her that Elizabeth, her much older cousin, was miraculously pregnant as well. Once Mary moved from a place of fear to faith, she accepted the responsibility of partnering with God to change the world through her pregnancy.

What happened next has always moved me because it speaks to the power of women coming together. Instead of isolating herself and waiting for the miracle to become a reality, she went to see her cousin Elizabeth. I believe the angel Gabriel made it a point to make sure that Mary knew someone understood the responsibility of being a force with a miracle in the making.

Some battles we must face alone, but in other battles we

must resist isolation if we're going to have victory. Pay attention to the moments when God places someone in your world who is walking a similar path as you. There is power in joining forces with someone who is determined not to miss anything God has for them.

You may be looking for friends who share similar interests, and that's okay. But when it comes to your destiny and the battleground where your fear and faith are facing off, you need someone who understands the power of God to make something happen that others deemed impossible.

When we take advantage of the wisdom available to us from those God has placed in our lives, it is not a sign of weakness—it is a show of unstoppable force.

## LAY IT DOWN

I open my heart to embrace the moments God sets people in my path who are traveling the same direction I am.

# 36 Unnatural Trust

Make me truly happy by agreeing wholeheartedly with each other, loving one another, and working together with one mind and purpose.

PHILIPPIANS 2:2 NLT

**IN NATURE, THERE IS A PHENOMENON THAT INVOLVES** two flows coming together to create a more powerful force. It's called a *confluence*. Geography teaches us that a confluence is when two rivers join together in order to form a single channel. When this single channel forms, the two rivers no longer exist as singular flows, but two streams have come together to create an even more powerful current.

The most famous example of this is the Amazon River. The two rivers that join together to make the Amazon River are the Solimões River and the Rio Negro. I can't help but marvel at the irony that the Amazon River is more known than either of the two rivers that join to form it in the first place. You already know that as a preacher I can't pass up the lesson in this moment. It's possible that what's on the other side of partnership is so undeniably powerful that every version of who you were before the confluence is small in comparison.

Imagine, if you can, what would have happened had the two rivers never converged. Nothing necessarily indicates that the rivers would have dried up or become depleted. No evidence suggests that the two rivers would've gotten stronger individually and gone on to rival the impact of the Amazon River.

If we personify these rivers, we can imagine they would have had to confront and overcome the many societal and personal barriers that deter us from converging with other forces. Fear of losing individualism and distinction or the concern that they weren't as qualified as the other river may have been realities. In geography, confluence is involuntary, but not so much in our spiritual, emotional, and relational journeys.

Too often we run the risk of staying in the flow of being individual rivers. We're so content with staying in our own flow that we miss out on the unique gift that occurs when two forces come together. Connecting with another person who is moving with the same sense of purpose, destiny, peace, and power as you is how humans experience confluences. Even deeper, merging our lives with God's will is a more transformational "river" than any confluence on earth, and that can be just as scary as intertwining our being with another person.

Joining forces with another person requires that we confront the fear of being lost in their story. Even once a person has shown themselves aligned with our values and intentions and proven that they can add strength to us in areas where our best could become better, the joining relies on an unnatural trust. I wonder what would happen if we actively engaged with the people in our world by analyzing whether the proposed engagement is forming a confluence or zapping us of power.

Qualifying our inner circle with a measuring stick of confluence is not about taking advantage of people. It's about understanding and valuing what you bring to the table. It's not as challenging to evaluate the ways a person can make you better as it is to determine the ways you can add value to them. That's why it's critical to have a healthy knowledge of your flaws and strengths.

## LAY IT DOWN

I have the ability to add value no matter what I've gone through.

## 37 Rushing Stream

> A river watering the garden flowed from Eden; from there it was separated into four headwaters.
>
> GENESIS 2:10 NIV

**ALMOST ALL OF THE OLD TESTAMENT FOLLOWS THE PATH** of two rivers desperately attempting to create a confluence to change the earth. The river of humanity and divinity engaged in a tangled waltz that often yielded disappointment.

No matter how much God desired to truly dwell with His people, His people could not trust that their partnership with God was more than enough without additions. The beauty of the New Testament is the lengths that God was willing to go for His creation to experience the ultimate confluence.

If we can truly wrap our minds around merging with God, we will understand the foundational framework for every relationship we possess. Live in the reality that the all-powerful, all-knowing, and ever-present God desires to dwell with you. He is there regardless of your weaknesses, ignorance, or disengagement.

The acceptance of that truth is humbling and convicting. It renders you vulnerable because God would rather have a trickle from you than nothing at all. He longs to unleash a divine stream of love and wisdom that radically changes your identity. If you're like me, it makes you feel overwhelmingly loved and undeserving.

Your job is not to get God to change His mind about you. Your job is to search God's mind for His truth about you. How do you search the mind of God? Of course, you can study how God engages with His creation in Scripture. That has proven to be incredibly instrumental for me.

There is another, more intimate option, however, that relies on your vulnerability. You must begin by assessing the areas where your mind disagrees with what you've heard about or experienced from God. Where is the disconnect between who you understand God is and who you are? When you begin to confront the area where there is separation between you and God, you directly attack the space that doubt, fear, and dark forces exploit.

For example, many people struggle to believe that God is good all of the time because not everything in their lives has felt good. This struggle is intensified the more they engage in choices they define as not being good. The problem is that when it becomes difficult to believe God is good, it also becomes nearly impossible to fully, truly trust God's plan for your life.

If that disconnect becomes the starting point for a journey of seeking and finding, it opens your heart to receive the wisdom of God's goodness and how it has shown up in your life even when you didn't see it.

Saying "God is good" is not the same as saying "life is good." God being good is the realization that good has a source, and the source is God. The substance of what God is made of is so good that even when good faces off against evil, it still turns out good.

When good takes over, doubt has to leave, bad loses its sting, the battles are no longer yours, and obedience is not a chore but a privilege because you trust where you're headed. When good takes over, it empowers you even when life isn't going as planned because you recognize that your life is not your own, but a confluence of God's goodness and your weakness working together so that heaven can touch earth.

## LAY IT DOWN

My invitation to God to meet me, no matter where I am, is inviting good to take over my life.

## 38 Searching in the Dark

> It is the glory of God to conceal a matter, but the glory of kings is to search out a matter.
>
> PROVERBS 25:2

**WHEN YOU DRAW CLOSER TO GOD, IT DOESN'T JUST INITI**ate a journey of bearing God's image on earth; it also grants you access to God's plans for the earth. Today's scripture from Proverbs sums this up perfectly and gives us insight into how God functions. Of course, when we think through the lens of our personal experiences, it's not a complete shock that God conceals things. Lord knows there have been plenty of moments when I've been completely in the dark about God's plans.

When I set aside the time, though, to truly seek the Holy Spirit in those dark seasons, I often find wisdom about why God allowed them, or didn't intervene, when I was at my lowest. Sometimes what you're calling darkness, God is calling development. It's the second part of this scripture that intrigues me because it puts the onus on an individual to not accept that darkness is the end.

When you refuse to believe that you serve a God who would leave you in the dark, you search scriptures, sermons, worship songs, and meditations until you begin to see light flickering again. The pursuit of God's perspective is not just about reconciling your past and making peace with your present. God's perspective also carries with it innovation for how your gifts and talents align with what God wants to see happen on the earth.

In communities of faith, it's not uncommon to hear someone share that God "spoke" to them. The concept leaves a lot of room for questions. Hearing from God is not the same as the phone ringing or a ping going off to let you know a message has come through. Fine-tuning your heart and spirit to understand when God is speaking takes intentionality and time.

I remember as a child some awkward moments when I'd accompany my parents to an event with their friends. Random men and women would approach me and marvel at how I'd grown. There's something powerful about someone knowing you long before you knew you. The sincerity in their words when they connect the characteristics they witnessed in your youth to the superpowers in your adulthood can be affirming and validating in ways you didn't even realize you needed.

These encounters are similar to what happens when we begin to truly experience a relationship with God. I'm going to give you a powerful thought to pray and meditate on as you begin to see how your very existence is an indication that God was innovating when He made you.

If you need evidence to ground my claim, you don't have to look any further than the reality of your DNA. The imprint of you that began formulating in your mother's womb was God curating an identity for you that would be unlike anything the world had ever seen. You were cutting-edge long before you took your first breath.

Embrace the truth that your existence is innovation. Your ideas that feel weird, quirky, and maybe a little strange are actually evidence that you're allowing your mind the freedom to live outside of constructs that exist to create conformity.

## LAY IT DOWN

I can move toward becoming more comfortable with letting my mind run wild without fear of rejection.

## 39 Bridge to a Miracle

"Send them away, that they may go into the surrounding country and villages and buy themselves bread; for they have nothing to eat." But He answered and said to them, "You give them something to eat."

MARK 6:36–37

**RESEARCH HAS SHOWN THAT ALLOWING OURSELVES TIME** to be bored is the best way to ignite our minds and imagination. We are overstimulated from the moment we wake up to the second we lie back down.

Most of our stimulation is the by-product of us living within the confines of someone else's imagination. You will never discover the power of your own ideas if you're constantly trapped in someone else's. Even if it's just for ten minutes a day, challenge yourself to direct your creativity in the direction of infinite possibilities.

I am reminded of when the disciples presented Jesus with a problem: a soon-to-be-hungry multitude of five thousand. They didn't even count how many women and children were there, and I'm not sure why because there's nothing more chaotic than a hungry woman and child. The disciples wanted Jesus to send them away, but Jesus refused and told the disciples to feed them instead.

The fellas drew a blank. They had no idea how they were supposed to respond to what seemed to be an impossible request, but because Jesus said they could do it, they had to take a minute and stretch their minds toward the possibilities they might have never considered. Jesus did not just want them to solve a problem with what had already been done. He wanted them to solve a problem with what had never been done before. To be a true disciple of Jesus, you must consider that the solution to a problem you do see may exist in a realm you do not see. It's not enough to see a problem if you don't trust that God has a solution worthy of searching His heart for.

The miracles in the Bible often involved the use of something already in reach. It's true you don't know how God is going to solve the problems you see, but what if you started seeing everything in your life as a bridge to a miracle? How differently would you treat it? What peace would be immediately available to you? Take the time to start wildly imagining the possibilities, and please note that the solution may be just as crazy as the problem. If you don't believe me, remember the disciples took a little boy's lunch and still had leftovers.

It's not enough to have the idea if you're not going to take the time to let your mind and hands wander into the possibilities of how to make it happen. I'm not trying to pull anyone's résumé, but I'm sure the people behind the invention of the flying vehicle didn't just have the idea but also the skills to turn it into a reality.

For most of us, the idea was nothing more than a random thought that scrolled through our minds, but for someone else, it launched a deep dive into a world of mechanics and engineering that produced a design so comprehensive that the FDA approved it for flight time. I am trying to help you unlock the confidence that allows you to see that complicated problems often have equally complex solutions. Don't let that discredit the power of your curiosity to pave the way for innovation.

## LAY IT DOWN

I have the opportunity to innovate in my day-to-day life as it relates to my interpersonal relationships, financial and time management, and wellness goals.

## 40 Reframe That Complaining

> Do everything without complaining and arguing, so that no one can criticize you.
> PHILIPPIANS 2:14–15 NLT

**I'M OFTEN LAUDED BY MY FRIENDS AND FAMILY FOR MY** patience. I usually think nothing of it, but I've come to pay attention to when I feel particularly impatient, and it doesn't happen often. When it does happen, usually one thing is the culprit: complaining.

I. Am. Not. A. Fan. I have one husband, six children, two parents, and four siblings, and I lead a team of a few dozen people. Suffice it to say, I have not found a way to rid my environment of complaining. Instead, I've learned to get to the root of why it irritates me and pray that God grants me more patience.

One of the reasons I complain is I expect people to not just be vocal about what's wrong, but to offer ideas on how to make it right. Even if the answer isn't workable or feasible, if you stop at complaining, you've just dumped a problem onto my already full plate.

God is working on my patience by having me challenge the person who's presented a problem to be innovative in finding a solution. It works like a charm when I'm able to do it without an attitude. When my seven-year-old comes to me in a panic because her older siblings won't spend time with her, I don't minimize her feelings or distract her with something else to do. I guide her in giving expression to what she feels so that she has the capacity for innovation.

How many times have you settled into rejection when there's an opportunity for you to stretch your mind into possibilities?

What power and talents are lying dormant in you because you've allowed a complaint to become a conclusion? Innovation is not a one-time thing reserved for the next big invention. Innovation is a muscle that we have the opportunity to exercise each day if we're willing to think outside of defeat. Your mind is the most powerful weapon you possess. When nurtured properly, it can empower you to unlock limitless potential. With all its power, it's still relatively fragile, and with one experience or thought, you can find yourself distrusting of yourself and stagnant.

When you transition to living with an innovation mindset, the impossible no longer feels too out of reach.

You'll know that your innovation has the potential to be fruitful when it is rooted in gratitude for the present and in the passion to transform the future problems before they even arise with solutions. When you innovate from a place of peace, your power maintains a healthy flow. You'll notice that as you begin to expand your mind with innovative thinking, your thoughts won't be the only things that change.

Your conversations will change too. When that happens, your social circle may also change. I probably should have warned you before I started sharing about changing your mind, but better late than never to inform you that a transitioned mind must often say goodbye.

## LAY IT DOWN

The problems I see are opportunities to stretch my mind toward establishing new pathways for efficiency and success.

## 41 Flowing with Others

> Let us consider how we may spur one another on toward love and good deeds.
>
> HEBREWS 10:24 NIV

**WHEN PEOPLE ARE TRYING TO GET TO KNOW YOU, THEY** are trying to determine what type of person you are. Once they've identified your type—shy, fashionable, athletic, smart, fun-loving, clumsy, funny, forgetful, moody—they build walls around you and expect you to stay in the categories they understand.

It is crucial for you to fully comprehend the reality of your inheritance of power through your relationship with Jesus. When you refuse to live within the box that people have relegated you to, you cultivate relationships that are as fluid as the power you flow in.

Imagine there are two types of people in your life: people who flow with your power and people who can only handle one version of you. Believe it or not, they are both equally necessary for your spiritual health and well-being.

Let's use Jesus as an example. The disciples consistently stayed with Jesus throughout His ministry. The disciples weren't just observers of what was happening in His life. They also weren't sycophants chasing the clout of His fame.

The disciples were connected to Jesus because being in His flow awakened them to the possibilities of how their connection with God was a river waiting to be released into the earth. Before Jesus chose his disciples, though, He had His mother, Mary. She flowed with Jesus up until His ministry began, then we see a shift.

The woman who once flowed with Him was now floating sporadically throughout the scenes of His life. She was not as constant as the disciples, but occasionally we see her in pivotal moments. Mary gave Jesus the space He needed to innovate without requiring Him to stay accessible.

It wasn't until Jesus stepped into the fullness of His ministry that disruption in His connection with Mary occurred. Disruption is not always dysfunction; sometimes it's a sign of development. It's impossible to stay the same and change simultaneously. When Jesus went from possessing power to releasing power, it changed His connections in His social circle.

When you begin to put your power out there, you will be sounding an alarm to your friends, family, and community that the current of who you once were is shifting, and you're flowing differently than you were before. When your innovation transitions from being more than a silly passing idea to a powerful plan in motion, you will be able to see clearly who can flow with you and who will be a member in your village who can't go with you but has enough wisdom to not hold you back.

Someone who can flow with you studies how you communicate, interact, disseminate, and retain your power so that they can support, expand, and restore you in the way you need it the most. The disciples were not just along for the ride. They were changing the tires, filling up the tank, cleaning the windows, and ready to get behind the wheel if necessary.

I won't lie to you and say it's easy to have peace when the people you wanted to flow with you make it evident that, at most, all they can do is float by occasionally. But there is something to be said about trusting that the obedience God is requiring of you is worth the discomfort of flowing anyway.

## LAY IT DOWN

God will bring the right people at the right time to help me accomplish every plan He has for my life.

## 42 Proactive Communication

Sympathize with each other. Love each other as brothers and sisters. Be tenderhearted, and keep a humble attitude.

1 PETER 3:8 NLT

**ABANDONING YOUR COMFORT ZONE AND FOLLOWING GOD** is hard work. It requires a lifelong commitment of living a vulnerable life. Seeing other people stuck in the crosshairs of fear and indecision makes you more sympathetic than judgmental.

Tapping into transformation, regardless of where you're starting from, is an opportunity to be more delicate with people who are still finding their way. When you truly recognize how arduous the process of being renewed and restored by God is, it should make you a safe space for others.

From a place of true humility, you're able to recognize that you may be the one floating while someone you once felt close to flows on by. There will come a time when your idea must be shared with someone. You need valuable input with various perspectives to help you understand what part of your concept is viable and what's underdeveloped. We all have blind spots, and input offers a more thorough view of how to position what's in our hearts to have the maximum impact in the world.

Whoever you're in relationship with is an individual so unique that their fingertips and DNA cannot be replicated. Why would we force a cookie-cutter way of connecting, loving, and supporting onto someone whom God has graced with that level of distinction?

When we choose to innovate in the ways of love, we're daring to ask the person we're committed to how to best show up in a way that matters the most to them. There's not a classroom more skilled at teaching innovative relational skills than parenting.

All it takes is more than one child for you to realize that what worked for one won't work for the other. I'm learning to make space for my individuality while protecting, serving, and developing my little humans into good people. Even though I'm a busy mom with a demanding travel schedule, I don't want my children's gifts and talents to be stifled by my schedule.

As a result, I end up saying no to more things than I say yes to, but there are still trips, projects, and tasks I enjoy that take me away from them. Do I feel guilty for that? Sometimes. But I'm also honest enough to admit that there are moments when I've felt bitter because I denied my needs in order to be the kind of mom I'm "supposed" to be.

In a perfect world I'd attend every practice, rehearsal, recital, tournament, and presentation while also attending meetings, recording podcasts, finishing manuscripts, preaching sermons, and developing new ideas.

Well, the world isn't perfect, and there's no way I can check all of the boxes. The first step in introducing innovation into my rhythm as a mother was communication. I discovered that I was often communicating from a place of burnout instead of being proactive about my capacity in advance.

Proactive communication begins with yourself. You have to be willing to look at all of your tasks and responsibilities and determine what you desire to accomplish versus what you legitimately have the capacity to accomplish. I know you would do it all if you could, but you also know you can't do it all.

## LAY IT DOWN

The sooner I can be honest with myself about what's possible, the more quickly I can connect with those around me who can offer me support.

## 43 Grace to Survive

> From the end of the earth I will cry to You, when my heart is overwhelmed; lead me to the rock that is higher than I.
>
> PSALM 61:2

**I KNOW A THING OR TWO ABOUT RUNNING OUT OF GAS.** The crazy part is that even though the car doesn't move, it doesn't mean it has no power. I want you to know that just because you have the power to start something doesn't mean you'll always have the fuel it takes to make sure it's complete.

Checking your inner fuel tank is a practice that sets the tone for your day, but the sooner you can get ahead of it, the better. If you're able to look at your life a couple of days or even a week in advance, you're able to better pace yourself. Once you assess what's realistic for you to accomplish, you can readjust expectations of those affected—and that's when the innovation begins.

You get to go through each task and ask yourself, *Do I really have to do this, or am I doing it because it's what I'm supposed to do?* There's a moment in the Bible where Adam told God that he was hiding because he was naked, and God asked him, "Who told you that you were naked?" (Genesis 3:11). However you imagine God asking that question is how I want you to ask yourself, *Who told you you're supposed to do it this way?*

The questions you're asking are meant to restore your power as an individual, not a puppet. They are meant to serve you in assessing whether you are living up to your idea of what a business owner, partner, friend, or family member should be or trying to force yourself to fit in the construct your community created. Here's your chance to innovate!

More often than not, I've found myself seeking to become

powerful at being who others perceive me to be instead of living in the power of my truth and authenticity. Counterfeit power is built on the validation of many. Real power can exist only when we flow in who God has called us to be.

Welcoming innovation into the dynamics of how you relate with others eliminates the need to give yourself or others ultimatums. Innovation is the gateway for compromise that feels mutually beneficial and not like one person got the short end of the stick. It helps to ensure that relationships maintain their equity and closes the gap for burnout.

You have a lot going on in your world, and you're not always going to get it right. As a matter of fact, there will be moments when there's no room for innovation, and all you can do is pray for the grace to survive the days ahead. In those moments I want to challenge you to get innovative with your prayers.

Take the time to communicate with yourself and size up your responsibilities. But instead of turning to an individual to help, ask God, with specificity, to send His Spirit to guide you in the places you fear depletion.

## LAY IT DOWN

When my capacity does not measure up to the responsibilities at hand, I get to ask the Holy Spirit to fill my cup and order my steps.

# 44 On Assignment

> You are a chosen people, a royal priesthood, a holy nation, God's special possession, that you may declare the praises of him who called you out of darkness into his wonderful light.
>
> 1 PETER 2:9 NIV

**YOUR LIFE HAS A PREDETERMINED IMPACT THAT IS MEANT** to fill the world with love and goodness no matter how much pain and bitterness you have experienced. Your life matters to God's master strategy of reconciling His creation back to Him.

The foundation of my faith is connected to my profound belief that following the life of Jesus is the only way to experience the fullness of God's plan for the earth and for you. When we model our lives after Jesus, as children of God, we no longer represent just ourselves, but God too.

We become part of what Scripture calls a royal priesthood, and that makes us ambassadors of heaven who are on assignment on earth. It's like joining a branch of the armed forces. No matter where you are from or who you were connected with before, what matters most is the assignment connected to your enlistment.

Jeremiah 1:5 lets us in on how God connects with His creation before they even take their first breath. Once we enter the world and are exposed to all of the things that make life beautiful and complicated, we have no recollection of those moments before our mother's womb. Yet many of us come to suspect that there is more to life than the moment we're drowning in. The pursuit for salvation comes in many forms. Some find it in achievement. Others find it in drugs. Then there are the ones who look for it in alcohol. And let's not forget about the ones who try to find it in love.

We find different saviors along the way, but none leaves us satisfied; we must discover true relationship with Jesus. I love an authentic church with trustworthy leadership, but that's not finding Jesus. A relationship with Jesus is a fully integrated faith that begins with a curiosity, a "trial" period, and then finally a real commitment.

I think it's important we acknowledge these stages because when I was growing up, I perceived that if I could not be on fire for God, there was no space for my flicker at all. So I want you to know what I learned later in life. For some, walking with Jesus is an overnight inferno that completely consumes their lives. Then there are those of us whose walk with Jesus begins with sentences like, "If You're real, help me to really feel Your presence." What's crazy is how I started uncertain and unsure, but now I know, without a doubt, that the power of God has shown up in my life in a way that cannot be explained away.

Jesus already knows you're imperfect. He isn't expecting perfection. He could not care less about your dirty little secrets. For some crazy reason, Jesus calls our scars beautiful and longs to see our slates wiped clean.

Nothing is more powerful than being radically loved by Someone who is not surprised by your success and is compassionate when you're at your worst.

## LAY IT DOWN

When having a faith that feels certain is out of reach, a small mustard seed is enough for God to start working with.

## 45 Willing to Risk It All

Well done, good and faithful servant; you have been faithful over a few things, I will make you ruler over many things. Enter into the joy of your lord.

MATTHEW 25:23

**IN MATTHEW 25 JESUS SHARED A PARABLE ABOUT THE** kingdom of heaven. The authority figure was a master with three servants. The chapter shares with us that the servants were each given "talents."

Before you start thinking that the master gave one impeccable rhythm and another the voice of an angel, that's not what *talent* means in this instance. The word translated "talent" in the New King James Version was later translated "bags of gold" in the New International Version of the Bible.

Even without the translation, reading the full account of the parable makes it pretty clear that the servants were given some type of currency, and they were expected to take what they were given and multiply it through investment. Two of the three servants were successful at multiplying their talents. The one who failed to increase the talent he was given was not unsuccessful because of a lack of effort.

The man was unsuccessful out of extreme caution. He did not want to risk losing what he'd been given and determined that at least returning what he had was better than taking the risk of losing it altogether. While I do believe there's something to be said about being a good steward of your finances and understanding how investments can make your money work for you, I believe the principle Jesus was sharing here is much deeper.

I perceive that Jesus was trying to teach us about the risk

we must be willing to take to be fruitful in spreading the revelation of the kingdom of heaven. The principle that power is not reserved for a select few but is freely given to anyone willing to be led by the Spirit of God is not just a good idea—it's a revelation. The reality that your past does not define you and that Jesus doesn't just look past your flaws but literally looks right at them and still thinks you're to die for is a revelation.

This parable is showing us that the kingdom of heaven is like a master, God, who gave His servants, us, something that is too valuable to keep to ourselves. If you know that what you have comes from God, but you keep it within because you're afraid to fail, you are allowing what God has given you to bow down to fear. Jesus does not want us to hoard what we've been given.

God can't multiply what you won't sacrifice. The man with the talents was so afraid of failing that he missed the opportunity for multiplication. When the other servants proved they could take what they'd been given and multiply it, they showed their master they could endure the vulnerability that comes with risking failure.

The Greek word translated "talents" in Matthew 25 actually means "weight." In ancient Rome, money was not counted by dollars and cents but by weight.

The man who did not increase his talents ultimately did not add more weight to what the master had given him. The ones who were celebrated received praise because they managed to take the weight given to them and make that weight work for them.

## LAY IT DOWN

When I surrender my "talents" to God to be used for His glory, He multiplies them to touch the lives of those around me.

## 46 My Weight to Carry

> Each one should test their own actions. Then they can take pride in themselves alone, without comparing themselves to someone else, for each one should carry their own load.
> GALATIANS 6:4–5 NIV

**EACH OF US ENTERS THIS WORLD WITH A WEIGHT TO BEAR.** Some of us may have only one burden while others may have so much of a load that it's bearing down on their shoulders. We all have moments when we become so distracted by what we're carrying that we miss out on the opportunity to make it work for us.

What if we spent less time trying to get rid of the weight we're carrying and more time trying to figure out why God chose us to carry it in the first place?

In the parable of the talents, we learn more than a principle about what's expected of us when we're part of the kingdom of heaven. We also learn that when we act like the man with one talent, we're seeing ourselves less than how God sees us. The master was upset because he knew that the servant had what it took to let that weight turn him into a heavyweight.

You need a mindset that clings to the belief that failure is not a blemish on your résumé but a brick on the road to your destiny. You are going to fail. You're going to be brilliant at some things and terrible at others. You're going to start off terrible in something and become a master the more you practice.

I need you to begin to see past the devastation of failure and instead see it as a necessary tool that God uses to construct who He knows you can become. One of the many lessons from this parable is that what feels like a risk to you may be the only way you truly get to experience all God's placed inside you.

I marvel at Jesus' ability to straddle the duality of His existence. He was completely human and completely divine. His ability to master living at this intersection should be the goal of how we spend our time on earth. It's only possible when we are fully convinced of the divine necessity of our life on earth. I will never get tired of reminding some and informing others that their lives are not random. You were not created out of boredom or haphazardly.

The context of your birth doesn't matter. Everything that God created has a purpose in His creation. Your father or mother may not have known what to do with you, but that doesn't change the fact that God has use for you. The tension of not being completely understood by the people in our environments is a source of trauma until we recognize that it's often why we triumph.

If you were completely understood, you would never seek to be exposed to environments that reflect externally what you feel internally. The hunt is ultimately the beginning of what allows us to truly tap into the image of God that we were designed to reflect.

## LAY IT DOWN

The greatest gift I can give the people I love is the freedom to grow without being limited by my perceptions.

## 47 Present and Open

> God is love, and he who abides in love abides in God, and God in him.
>
> 1 JOHN 4:16

**LOVE IS NOT JUST ACCEPTING SOMEONE FOR WHO THEY** are; it's also accepting them for who they are becoming. I'm not sure it's possible to love someone with this type of dexterity unless you fully embrace that this kind of love is available in your relationship with God.

Jesus modeled this love in the way He connected with the people He encountered in His ministry. He was able to be fully present with their suffering and fully hopeful for their future restoration. Jesus didn't just straddle the line of humanity and divinity; He also straddled the line of the present and the future. I want us to learn to do the same.

Jesus knew His journey was leading to the cross, but He did not shun all of the people, opportunities, and experiences on the way. Imagine Jesus ignoring the blind man yelling from the side of the street, the woman with the issue of blood, the men with leprosy, or any of the other miracles He performed.

Imagine if Jesus would've waited to find an empty cross and convinced someone to help Him fulfill the mission so He could just check the box as complete. It sounds ridiculous, because at the end of the day Jesus was not just meant to die for our sins. He served as an example of what a reconciled life with God looks like. Jesus had a focus on the future while remaining sensitive to the lessons hidden in each day.

While God is still revealing the plans and strategy for your future, you must trust and believe that the clues are hidden in your present. A healthy relationship with disappointment and failure is critical in assuming a posture of power while you're waiting on God's plan to unfold.

If your failures could change God's mind about you, He would never have sent His Son to save you. Each day—whether it's a day when your incompetence and inadequacy are on full display or a day when you feel so powerful you're shocking yourself—is an opportunity to ask God what He's trying to show you about His character or yours.

When we straddle this fence in our relationships, it allows us room to be frustrated but committed. I can be upset about what you did and in love with who you are. I can be intent on building what God's given me and compassionate toward those who don't understand it yet. The polarization that exists in most societies, and heavily in American culture, has caused many of us to believe that if we aren't choosing sides, we can't be effective.

We are to be in the world but not of it. That means there will be moments when we learn through mistakes and failure that we were leaning too far in one direction. Hindsight is a teacher that helps you see clearly how to show up in power for your future.

Trust that the only win in life is reflecting God's image on earth. Don't allow your win to be determined by how well you perform. Instead, lean into a mindset of victory anchored in how many lessons you've learned. When you are anxious for nothing, you're able to be present in the moment and open for the impossible.

## LAY IT DOWN

Instead of seeing disappointment and failure as a delay or denial, I get to see them as divinely assigned to develop me.

## 48 Taking Responsibility

Confess your sins to each other and pray for each other so that you may be healed.

JAMES 5:16 NLT

**MOST OF US ARE FAMILIAR WITH THE HIPPOCRATIC OATH.** It holds physicians to a standard of ethics that seeks to serve each patient with wisdom, compassion, and innovation.

It is my wholehearted belief that most physicians who take this pledge do so with the intent of truly serving their patients to the best of their ability. I imagine that as technology and science have advanced, the medical field has been able to deepen its commitment to the philosophies expressed in the oath. I also realize there's another truth neither patient nor doctor can avoid: Viruses and diseases are advancing and becoming more complicated almost at the same rate as technology and science—sometimes surpassing them. That's why doctors keep ever present the reality that they are yet practicing.

Though they take a vow to do no harm, they also recognize that the vow does not promise patients will always get the outcome they desire. It may not be the doctor's intent for the patient or family to experience harm in the process of their treatment, but intent and outcome are two separate experiences.

I've never met anyone who is a master at parenting, friendships, marriage, entrepreneurship, professional advancement, or academia. In many ways we're all practicing and hoping for the best results. Like a doctor, the potential exists for life-altering results as a result of our practice.

Acknowledging that level of pressure can be crippling and deflating. I don't want to practice at being a wife, mother, daughter, sister, friend, or leader. I want to be a master at them all. Still, it's clear that I am indeed practicing.

Many of us are learning to embrace the reality that we are not perfect; despite our best efforts, we're likely to fall short. But I'd like expand on this reality. You may not just fall short. You, regardless of your intent, may inflict harm on another individual. The power you move with can be transformed from a tool into a weapon and wound an undeserving soul.

Power without accountability will always turn into abuse. I believe this is why Jesus was intentional about taking time away from His close circle to have solitude with God. It wasn't just about the necessary refreshing and restoration that comes from connecting with God. Prayer is an opportunity for God to fine-tune our spirits when we've become detached from how our actions are negatively affecting the people in our lives.

When a doctor's practice has damaging outcomes, they are held accountable. When we have damaging outcomes, we're not always held accountable. Since most people have not been afforded the right to express disappointment without disconnection, they internalize or suppress the way our words and actions negatively affect them.

Of course, nothing we suppress or avoid actually goes away, and the inability to be held accountable negatively affects people we value and prohibits them from truly being able to grow in loving and serving the people they're in connection with.

Being seen by others with all of your beauty and flaws is one thing, but creating space for another imperfect person to share where you can be made whole is a skill that must be developed.

## LAY IT DOWN

Nothing is more powerful than being able to take responsibility for where I've messed up so I can grow.

## 49 Taking Feedback

> Each of you should use whatever gift you have received to serve others, as faithful stewards of God's grace in its various forms.
>
> 1 PETER 4:10 NIV

**WHO WAS YOUR FAVORITE TEACHER GROWING UP? DID** they teach a particular grade or subject? Chances are, you did not have the same teacher from kindergarten to fifth grade. I'll take it a step further and wager that you didn't have the same teacher from kindergarten to middle school or high school.

I wish I could attribute that to prophetic insight, but the truth is, I've connected with enough teachers to know it's very rare that a teacher has the desire or ability to teach every single subject of every single grade. It's not that they don't have the ability to increase their proficiency in order to cover more than one grade, but it's unlikely because they recognize that their teaching interest and style are more suitable for a certain subject and grade level.

I don't expect my daughter's history teacher to assist her with chemistry homework. He may be able to, but that's not a strength he's allowed us to observe. It would be foolish to believe that he's incapable of adding value at all just because that is not his strength.

It takes multiple teachers for a student to become a master. Likewise, it takes multiple teachers for a person to become a force. I want to prepare you for the reality that some of the teachers that God has assigned to your life are going to be imperfect. That may sound elementary, but it's important that you begin to accept that the teachers assigned to your life will also still be students in another area.

It's like an older sibling helping the younger with math. The older sibling is doing algebra, and the younger is doing addition. They're both still learning, but one has learned enough to help the other. We often miss the opportunity to gain the advantage on our brokenness because we reject teachers who are still in development.

I've had to wrestle with accepting feedback about my life from people who don't have their lives together. It's true that some people were definitely giving me advice they weren't taking themselves, but I've had to ask myself to look beyond the source and test the validity of the advice against my relationship with God.

The first few years of my marriage, I was notorious for doing this with my husband. I could not keep my mind from thinking on all of the ways he could adjust and become better.

I kept these thoughts to myself and allowed them to take up space in our marriage until finally I realized that the divide could be filled by gently showing one another the ways we unintentionally harm others. Deflecting from the way you harm someone and highlighting the way they harm instead is a sign of immaturity that keeps you from truly being powerful.

A person who is powerful doesn't need for their teacher to be perfect in order to challenge them to grow. There was only one perfect teacher, and He's sitting at the right hand of the Father. The rest of us are down here doing the best we can to turn our wounds into lesson plans. Sometimes God uses the people around you to develop the gift of God in you.

## LAY IT DOWN

I owe it to who I desire to be in God to consider the way other people experience me against the person I'm aiming to become.

## 50 Active Accountability

Encourage each other and build each other up, just as you are already doing.

1 THESSALONIANS 5:11 NLT

**REMEMBER WHEN WE TALKED ABOUT BEING INNOVATIVE** in the ways we relate? After you visualize that innovation and dare to enact it in your life, the next step is quality assurance. That's when you make sure you are living up to who you've set out to be among those you serve, lead, and connect with.

The only way to perform a quality assurance check is to open the lines of communication with direct questions. Instead of asking, "Do you think I'm a good friend?" ask, "Do you feel that I'm loyal to you and supportive of your work?" Asking targeted questions opens the door for rebuking and/or recalibrating.

Introducing opportunities for active accountability creates a culture in your relationship for feedback about the ways you can improve. When accountability is introduced, it lays a foundation for trust and safety between individuals. When a person knows you can handle the truth without punishing them for their experience, they feel safe enough to be authentic and corrected when needed.

Trust without accountability is an illusion. Exercising opportunities for accountability is the only way we can be reasonably sure that the people we're in relationship with are not suppressing in order to make things function. I'll be the first to let you know it won't always be easy to hear how your stress, insecurities, pride, or frustrations are negatively affecting the people in your life.

The question is, Would you rather hear about it or feel it in the way people slowly drift away? This process will make you vulnerable, and there will be moments when you will feel ashamed of the way you've acted or communicated. Once you survive the awkward vulnerability, you'll notice the roots of your relationship becoming deeper and richer.

Accountability produces an intimacy that can be experienced only when two individuals form a relationship where each is just as much teacher as student.

I've only heard the phrase *power forward* used in basketball, but it's the two words that came to mind when writing this entry. I'm not much of a basketball fan, so I won't attempt to draw a parallel between the basketball position and the thought God gave me. If you're a basketball fan, I'm going to ask that you please forgive me in advance for deliberately expanding the definition to prove this next point.

It takes just as much power to be held accountable for the way you cause harm as it does to move forward after you've been made aware of the ways you're still growing. Powering forward requires accepting the reality of your human frailty and being compassionate with yourself while maintaining your commitment to growth.

It's a little bit like rubbing your head and patting your stomach at the same time until you get into the rhythm of doing it. This is where stillness, intentional introspection, and an intimate prayer life become your healers and your weapons. They're weapons because they protect you from falling into an abyss of self-defeat, and they're your healers because they undergird a message that you will have to learn over and over: You can be powerful without being perfect.

## LAY IT DOWN

Being vulnerable and admitting where I have hurt others strengthens my relationships and promotes my own growth.

## 51 Strength in Our Weakness

> He gives power to the weak, and to those who have no might He increases strength.
>
> ISAIAH 40:29

**INTROSPECTION IS WHEN YOU TAKE THE TIME TO EXAM**ine your thoughts, emotions, and actions and recognize how they compete or align at any given moment. Through introspection we're able to understand that some of the ways we harm others are connected to unaddressed stress, fear, or anxiety.

Another person's feedback tells you what you did, but introspection helps you understand how you were feeling and what you were thinking when you did it. It is a powerful tool when accompanied with prayer because it allows us to pour our hearts out to God.

It's one thing to pray about what you did, but it's another to ask God to help you heal and express the thoughts that allowed it to occur in the first place. You'll notice through introspection that you'll go from being defensive when someone attempts to hold you accountable to validating their experience because of the knowledge of the state you were in when the harm occurred.

The only way forward after you've caused harm is to reclaim the power of your weakness. You can allow your weakness to be what isolates and restricts you from connection, or you can see weakness as a runway. When a plane is getting ready to take off, it seems like everything has come to a halt. The plane is aligned in the lane, passengers are buckled up, and the flight attendants have stopped moving about. Those few seconds of stillness give way to the roar of engines, and suddenly the plane begins to move at full throttle into the limitless sky.

When weakness becomes your runway, your only job is to hang tight to the truth that a momentary halt is not failure. It is your opportunity to recalibrate and rev up with more determination, focus, and power than you had before. I know you're probably wondering how it's even possible to accomplish such a task when the weight of your guilt, disappointment, or rejection feels too heavy to bear. I've got a scripture to help you with that.

It's 2 Corinthians 12:7–9, and it was written by the apostle Paul. He was sharing with a church in Corinth what Jesus said to him when he admitted to struggling with the fact that he was undeniably anointed and called. Yet on the other hand, he was so well acquainted with his weakness that he called it a "thorn in the flesh" (v. 7).

This is how Paul said Jesus responded to his dilemma: "And He said to me, 'My grace is sufficient for you, for My strength is made perfect in weakness.'" Paul's response to the knowledge of Jesus' strength being made perfect in him is revealed in the second part of the verse when Paul shared, "Therefore most gladly I will rather boast in my infirmities, that the power of Christ may rest upon me" (v. 9).

When you feel like powering down altogether, remember this scripture. Remember that you can withstand the process of development that allows the power of Christ to rest upon you. Recognize that the promises of God over your life can be voided only if you allow your fear to cancel them out.

Don't allow the fact that you messed up to keep you down. If you're going to make a mistake, allow those moments to highlight just how far you are from being like God and how gracious God has been in extending you grace to make up the difference.

## LAY IT DOWN

The power of Christ rests on me and makes up the difference in the places where I fall short.

## 52 What We Impart

> Let your light shine before others, that they may see your good deeds and glorify your Father in heaven.
>
> MATTHEW 5:16 NIV

**WHEN I WAS GROWING UP, I THOUGHT THAT HAVING CHIL-** dren was just about being able to say you have a family. My journey with parenting began when I was a teenager, so I learned on the job that parenting is really about raising future adults who love Jesus and are knowledgeable and confident enough to add indisputable value to their corner of the world.

Sure, I want to move with power, burn with confidence, and become a force. One of the best ways to test whether that is happening is not judged in how frequently I embody that desire but how often I impart to others when I am functioning from that place. When you can't avoid the moments when you feel low, you must control what you impart from the place of despair.

Some days you feel unshakable and determined; other times you feel unmotivated and in shambles. That's normal, but part of knowing your harm is recognizing that in those moments, what you share could be more than venting. It could actually be impartation.

*Impartation* is defined as "the act of imparting something (such as knowledge or wisdom)." The Latin etymology of the word *impart* indicates that the word means "in part." This means that when we are sharing anything, whether it be knowledge or wisdom, we're not just venting to another person; we are giving them a part of what we're going through.

This is why it's so important to understand whether the person on the receiving end of our words is capable of processing what we share with empathy, wisdom, and discernment. Otherwise, we'll be divulging a temporary frustration that has permanent implications because of who we divulged it to.

This concept is made even clearer when we consider the ways that we must exhibit discretion when communicating with children, coworkers, or family members with misaligned core values and perspectives. Not every person in your life is in a position to carry your pieces with integrity.

If as much is true for the delicate parts of our lives, how much more truth does it hold for our ability to impart power? When Jesus first encountered a random man fishing in a sea, He didn't lure him away with promises of riches or fame. He didn't convince him that love and a pain-free life awaited him. Jesus simply made him curious about how following Him could awaken an identity that he didn't know he possessed.

How much different would the world be if each person who has been awakened and enlightened to the power they have to effect lasting divine impact made it their mission to awaken and enlighten others?

Changing how we think about power is doing the work so that we can understand the multidimensional ways we experience and express power and share our findings with others who feel powerless. Don't gatekeep the areas where your power has been restored, lest you become like those who've led so many to believe that power is reserved only for a select few. The real sign of someone who is confident is not how they walk into the room. It's how they change every room they walk into for the better.

## LAY IT DOWN

It is my mandate to not just discover and harness my own power but to make sure I spread it to others.

## 53 Power in Proximity

> You have been called to live in freedom, my brothers and sisters. But don't use your freedom to satisfy your sinful nature. Instead, use your freedom to serve one another in love.
> GALATIANS 5:13 NLT

**IF HURT PEOPLE HURT PEOPLE, THEN EMPOWERED** people empower people. Jesus did not limit or restrict His impartation based on a person's experience or worthiness. Jesus was not afraid that by imparting power He'd run low on it. He understood that the more power you possess, the more you have to give away. Power is not in limited supply, and when you truly trust your connection to the all-powerful God, you're not a hoarder of power who sees other people struggling but refuses to fill their cups.

When a car's battery has been drained, the driver has to find cables to hook the dead battery up to a full battery to get a charge. I remember sitting in the back seat of cars in my childhood while that transfer of power took place. The charged car would rev the engine until the car that was dead eventually came back to life.

Impartation is aligning where you're charged with the place where another person is drained. Now, before you start worrying about how you'll fit all of this into your already busy life, let me guide you on the best way to make this a part of your world.

When a car battery dies, there are only two ways for another car to jump it. Another driver in proximity sees the struggling driver and asks if they can help by giving the car a jump. Or the person who needs a jump calls someone to help them.

In either scenario there's one common denominator: proximity. That should be part of the criteria that we use to gauge our ability to impart the power we've received into someone else's life. Too often when we think about change and impact, we think about the people we may not yet know who could benefit from the grace on our lives. This way of thinking discredits the opportunities.

I've heard a few people tell me that they've known since they were young that they were gifted and special. But for the most part, I hear testimonies of people who are wondering what sets them apart. They don't fully trust that there's anything about them worthy of distinction. In Jesus' time, being a fisherman was a common profession, but Jesus took what was common and bridged it to the supernatural. I bet Peter had no clue that his routine was actually the gateway for the supernatural.

I encourage you to begin asking God what He's placed inside you that could be a jump start to a person who is yet searching. Don't just take note of something that someone does well. Take the time to stress how special their offering is and how they can have greater impact than they realize.

You have to find a way to sow the power God's given you into the life of another person. Truly, Jesus shows us that power is not to be reserved but poured out into as many open and hungry vessels that one can reach. Intentionally create opportunities for other people to grow and develop. When you have the capacity, ask someone how you can use your resources to help them establish what God's doing in their life.

Locate the areas of your life where you have experienced the power of God in a way that feels unique. Then, like a car with a full battery, go and get next to someone who is dying in the place where you've been restored.

## LAY IT DOWN

I could be the spark someone needs to ignite their unique offering.

## 54 Give Freely

Do your best to present yourself to God as one approved, a worker who does not need to be ashamed and who correctly handles the word of truth.

2 TIMOTHY 2:15 NIV

**A MOMENT COMES WHEN YOU'RE NOT JUST GOING WITH** the flow anymore. You've actually become the flow. When someone encounters you, they're having a radical encounter with your authenticity and vulnerability. You should expect that you're carrying light with you wherever you go. So don't be be surprised when people begin to say that they feel better, calmer, more hopeful once they've been in your presence.

That is the by-product and overflow of what happens when we learn to seek the face of God and project God's face in all we see and do. God has given us methods of communication to spread our power that don't require us to go out of our way.

Sometimes we are so busy trying to make sure we pour into every person we meet that we don't take the time to observe if we're pouring into someone who is positioned to receive what we have to offer. When spreading power, it's important to understand what the traits are of the person who can maximize the resource of you in their life.

Has the person demonstrated the ability to truly convert wisdom and knowledge from other sources in the past? If you're just getting to know someone more intimately, avoid giving them everything you have at once. Only offer what you can afford to lose.

I cannot tell you how many times I've given someone the best of my thoughts, advice, and experiences only for them to do the direct opposite of what I'd suggested. I don't want to be one of those people who needs others to respond the way I see fit. My responsibility is to make sure that when I give, I'm able to give freely without being entitled to specific results.

If you're investing in a person with the unspoken requirement that they yield immediate transformation, it's actually manipulation. For the life of me, I will never understand why God gave His only begotten Son so that "whosoever" believes in Him could have everlasting life (John 3:16 KJV). If I gave my only child, you would not have an option on whether you believed. God demonstrates what it means to be a true giver. He gave His Son so that whosoever could have an option, not an obligation. I think this speaks to the heart posture in which God gave and the same perspective we should imitate when giving. God gave because of who He is, not because of what He wanted in return. That's what I want for myself. That's what I want for you.

I want to be able to give because giving is who I am, not because giving is a means to an end. If you want this to be your truth, too, you must be willing to know the limits of what you can give without expecting anything in return, not even a thank-you.

What can you afford to give regardless of whether someone appreciates it? That's the beginning of setting the boundaries for how you engage with others. This does not mean you don't give beyond that point, but it does mean that when you give beyond that point, you should be considering what type of response or reaction makes you feel like your investment was truly valued.

## LAY IT DOWN

Unleashing my light gives other people permission to do the same.

## 55 Sowing Generously

> God is the one who provides seed for the farmer and then bread to eat. In the same way, he will provide and increase your resources and then produce a great harvest of generosity in you.
>
> 2 CORINTHIANS 9:10 NLT

**HAVE YOU EVER HELD THE DOOR OPEN FOR SOMEONE TO** keep it from slamming in their face? Have you ever felt the mild irritation of them not saying thank you sting in the moment? No matter how frustrated that made you, I bet it didn't deter you from holding the door open for someone else. You know why? Because your conviction to demonstrate kindness in that way has more to do with who you are than how they respond.

I want to be clear: Spreading power is not just sharing the wisdom from some of your deepest wounds. You would be surprised how your norm could be empowering for someone else. Taking the time to make sure a person learns financial tools, communication tips, or time-saving practices that have helped you can serve them.

The advantage of being in community with one another is having opportunities to shorten the learning curve by sharing our experiences. You know you're truly confident when you're not threatened by someone else's access to what you have. At the end of the day, someone having your recipe doesn't mean they'll get your results.

As we continue to see the crumbling of systems and structures that historically excluded people groups, we must also confront the mentalities that made them successful in the first place. Subconsciously, many of us have been engrained to believe that only one of us can be in a space. If we believe there's only room for one woman, Black person, Latina person, young person, or old person, we do not actively seek to make room for others. There should be space for all types at every table, and it shouldn't be limited to any one group feeling like a minority. Dismantling the paradigm that there's only room for one helps us to be active participants in creating space for the next wave of people to come. Jesus did what only He could do, then He got twelve disciples and gave them power, too, because the depravity of the world was so great that even as powerful as Jesus is, His impact would be multiplied by others.

When Jesus gave them a charge, among the many things He said, this stood out: "Heal the sick, cleanse the lepers, raise the dead, cast out demons. Freely you have received, freely give" (Matthew 10:7–8). Considering the strict systems of separation by class and ethnicity at the time, Jesus must have understood the human proclivity to absorb power for personal gain instead of spreading power for the uplifting of many. His warning gives us perspective on how we should respond to the opportunity to elevate another soul.

When God has granted you the ability to be powerful on earth, it is not diminished by another person stepping into their power. You must become an advocate with a mindset that says, *We need as many people to win as possible so that we can shine with brilliance into dark places.* Lavishly share the hard-earned lessons you've learned with the people who are just starting off.

## LAY IT DOWN

The more people I sow into, the more opportunity I have for receiving a harvest of focused, intentional, and powerful beings.

## 56 What's the Root?

> Behold, you will be mute and not able to speak until the day these things take place, because you did not believe my words which will be fulfilled in their own time.
>
> LUKE 1:20

**LUKE 1 CONTAINS TWO TALES OF THE ANGEL GABRIEL'S** predicting the birth and significance of John the Baptist and Jesus. If we take a deeper look, we also learn the difference between doubt and curiosity.

Zacharias was a priest and a devout believer along with his wife, Elizabeth. His duty as a priest was to burn incense in the temple, a role of high significance that was part of a sacred religious ritual as people in the temple were praying. The angel Gabriel visited Zacharias at a time when he and Elizabeth were older in age and childless. Gabriel told Zacharias that his prayers to have a child were going to be answered—even specifying his unborn child's gender, describing the significance of his son and what his name would be.

As devout as Zacharias was and as much as he knew about God's faithfulness, his immediate response was rooted in doubt and human logic. He asked Gabriel how he would know this to be true. Zacharias was asking for evidence, as if he hadn't known God's history, His perfect track record of keeping His word. Zacharias allowed his faith to be overshadowed by human logic, and for this Gabriel told him that he would be unable to speak until the prophecy came to pass.

We shouldn't judge Zacharias for doubting because we do it too. We faithfully go to church on Sunday. We wake up before the sunrise to spend time in the Lord's presence. We have notes in our Bibles and believe the lyrics of our favorite worship songs, yet when God whispers the unthinkable to us, we doubt Him. We may not verbalize our doubt as Zacharias did, but it shows up in our hesitation to take a step of faith or our need for details.

Instead of judging Zacharias, we can learn from his doubt. Even seasoned believers who are intimately acquainted with the presence of God, knowing His works and faithfulness to His word, can struggle with trusting God when His plans seem improbable. Zacharias is an example of what happens when human logic competes with God's miraculous plan. God didn't allow Zacharias's doubt to derail His plan.

I find it interesting that God also didn't allow Zacharias's doubt to influence Elizabeth's faith. He literally couldn't speak about his experience until their son was born. He named him John as Gabriel had instructed even when others tried to talk him out of it.

Gabriel later visited Mary and told her that she would give birth to the Son of the Most High. She asked a question, too, but it was rooted in curiosity. She asked for a better understanding, rather than proof. Mary's response reflects a heart that is fully surrendered to God's will. Her faith shows that trust in God opens the door to His miraculous work.

True faith is not just believing in God's power but also submitting to His purpose. Mary didn't doubt Gabriel; she embraced her role in God's redemptive work. The angel's message was confirmed by Elizabeth's response to Mary's greeting: "Blessed are you among women, and blessed is the fruit of your womb!" (Luke 1:42).

When God's word falls on you, silence every doubt and allow curiosity to lead you to the fulfillment of His promise.

## LAY IT DOWN

I am learning to release doubt and embrace God's ability to perform goodness in and through my life.

## 57 Stepping into the Moment

God has not given us a spirit of fear and timidity, but of power, love, and self-discipline.

2 TIMOTHY 1:7 NLT

**HOW DO YOU BECOME A PERSON WHO STEPS INTO A** moment that feels bigger than you but is undeniably the place you're supposed to be?

A certain amount of fear is healthy. For example, when humans were a species who lived around wild animals, a certain amount of fear kept the lion from eating you and the snake from biting you. Fear can keep you from getting killed.

The Bible says, "God has not given us a spirit of fear" (2 Timothy 1:7), but a certain amount of fear is healthy. It's just that we don't want fear to drive. We want faith to drive. Fear might be in the trunk. It might even be in the back seat, but it's not what controls us.

The funny thing to me is that the contrast between the faith and the fear, the contrast between the spiritual and the carnal, and the contrast between the big mandate and the little me creates this feeling that is almost addictive. I feel alive only when I'm in front of a giant. My anointing doesn't kick in until it's something big enough to warrant the glory of God to fall.

I think that's why God puts us in big situations: so that we will depend on Him. Maybe you're facing a giant, maybe you're facing something that seems impossible, or maybe you're at your wit's end. God's grace is sufficient to keep you, carry you, strengthen you, and bring you to an expected end.

My friend, let's not stay in the shallow water. Let's go into the deep water, knowing He's going with us. The storm may rise and the lightning may flash and the boat may shake. But as long as Jesus is on board, we're going to get to the other side.

Sometimes you need to just exhale. Maybe every time you pick up your phone, you've got a certain anxiety. Even in your sleep you're bracing yourself. Take a moment to know you're in your heavenly Father's arms. You're in His care.

It's something we all need to do. When you're in a position of power over somebody, whether you're a mother or a businesswoman or a CEO, the fact that they admire you is a wonderful thing, but it also denies you the right to exhale because you don't want to let anybody down. You don't want to admit that you're tired or frustrated. You don't want to admit that you need some guidance and that you need to unload and that you can't go to Hawaii for three weeks like you want to. But in His presence, there is fullness of joy; at His right hand, there are pleasures forevermore (Psalm 16:11).

To be in the presence of God is rejuvenating. It is a vacation. It is restoration. It is renewal.

## LAY IT DOWN

I can take a deep breath and slowly exhale, resting in the knowledge that my heavenly Father holds me safely in His arms.

## 58 Let That Breath Out

> Then the LORD God formed a man from the dust of the ground and breathed into his nostrils the breath of life, and the man became a living being.
>
> GENESIS 2:7 NIV

**DO YOU SOMETIMES FEEL LIKE YOU'RE HOLDING YOUR** breath? Like you're drowning, so you've got to hold your breath just to survive? I think sometimes we hold our breath because we worry that if we release it, all the anger, frustration, fear, and disappointment we hold inside is going to come out.

Heaven knows that underneath all those emotions, God's glory is still in our breath. When God created man, He breathed His breath into him (Genesis 2:7). And if we want this world to see the fullness of who God is and the fullness of God's glory, then it's going to happen through our breath. So if we don't exhale what we've been holding on to, what has caused us to feel like we're drowning, then we may not get down to that base breath of glory, that base breath of peace.

God is uprooting all the things in my soul that have me feeling inadequate and insecure. He is saying, *I want to clear all that out of the way because when you get down to your last breath, your last breath is glory. And that last breath will sustain you for the rest of your life. That last breath will breathe into the next generation.*

He's clearing out what has been held within so that we can be the hands and feet of the Lord. We need to show up in our lives and our marriages and our communities and our businesses as the hands and feet of the Lord. If we don't come to a place within ourselves where we can exhale anything that is stuck to us, then we may miss the opportunity to establish the kingdom of heaven in our own families, our own hearts, our own ministries.

I want the kingdom of heaven to stand up in my life. So whatever other kingdoms I've been bowing to—the kingdom of fear, the kingdom of doubt—have to fade away so that the one true kingdom can be established and never torn down again.

Before there was a star—before there was a sun, moon, earth, sea, or atom—the very breath of God was there. That breath is what God gave Adam that made him a living soul (Genesis 2:7). Now, a lot of us are alive. We've got a pulse, but we're not living. Jesus said, "I have come that they may have life, and have it to the full" (John 10:10 NIV). He came that we might exhale so that we can inhale. When we can't exhale, we can't inhale what's next.

When you inhale, you're holding on to what was. But when you exhale, you release what was so that you can have capacity for what's next.

God has His hand on your life, and you are enough to handle whatever He calls you to do. You're gifted enough, you're talented enough, you're anointed enough, and you're called enough to deliver whatever He's going to do through you. It won't be you doing it anyway; it's going to come through you. Don't let the Enemy entangle you with any kind of uncertainty. Those whom God calls He qualifies. He equips you for what He's going to do in your life.

## LAY IT DOWN

God is able to bring me into alignment with who I need to be.

## 59 A Place of Increase

God is able to make all grace abound toward you, that you, always having all sufficiency in all things, may have an abundance for every good work.

2 CORINTHIANS 9:8

**WHEN A BABY IS BROUGHT IN FOR A CHECKUP, THE DOC-**tor asks questions that are meant to check on the baby's development. Can she sit up on her own? Is she able to handle the weight of her head? Is she rolling over? What the doctor is looking for are milestones of growth and development.

When the baby gets older and goes to school, the doctor considers her cognitive, emotional, and social development. How well does the child play with other children? Does she respond? Does she listen?

An interesting thing happens, though, when the child is older and has checked enough boxes. Doctors stop asking these questions. They stop asking if you're walking well on your own or holding your head up. Nobody cares if you're developing anymore.

That lasts for about two decades, until the doctor starts asking a different set of questions. Do you have any pain in your body that feels unfamiliar? Do you notice that your heart rate increases when you're doing things that used to be easy? These, too, are signs of development; they're just development in a different direction. This level of development is trying to assess where you are, trying to determine whether you're moving from a stage of stability to a stage of decline.

Often, when we hear the word *development*, we think about growth, expansion, and increase. But when researchers look at development, they define it in three different characterizations: growth, stability, and decline.

What's interesting is there is no announcement when you move from one stage to the next, and that's why you often need a doctor to ask you questions. They know what to look for even if you don't.

When a doctor looks at a baby and says she's a little behind for her age, he's able to offer intervention that can move the baby into a space of development that is more appropriate. Sometimes you can be increasing and not even realize it until someone tells you you're developing in an area.

When Jesus was at the wedding in Cana and the host ran out of wine, His mother nudged Him and told a servant to do whatever He said. Jesus responded, "Woman . . . My hour has not yet come" (John 2:4). But He performed the miracle anyway because Mary knew something about His development that Jesus hadn't realized yet. Scripture tells us that "Jesus increased in wisdom and stature, and in favor with God and men" (Luke 2:52). He was growing, but He also needed Mary to let Him know that what He had gone through was now ready to be released into the world.

Sis, I want you to know that you have developed enough to release what is inside you. The stage has been set, and sometimes you don't know that you have increased until someone lets you know you have developed enough to move into the next stage of your destiny. Sometimes you don't know it because you get so locked into the process that you settle into development forever, but there is a time when you move from growth into stability. And when you move from growth into stability, you may need someone to tell you that you've done enough reading; you've done enough listening; it's time for you to release what's inside you.

## LAY IT DOWN

Where is God inviting me into a place of increase?

## 60 Increase in Disguise

Oh, how great is Your goodness, which You have laid up for those who fear You, which You have prepared for those who trust in You in the presence of the sons of men!

PSALM 31:19

**INCREASE IS OFTEN DISGUISED. WE DON'T ALWAYS SEE IT.** When we increase, we don't always feel it. When we increase, that increase doesn't make an announcement. Sometimes we just look up and realize we're not who we used to be anymore because increase didn't let us know we were changing. We were just being obedient. We were just following the voice of God. We really weren't even looking for increase. We were looking to offer ourselves as a living sacrifice (Romans 12:1).

That's why we need someone to let us know when we have increase because, otherwise, we will think we are the same person we used to be. Sometimes we need someone to let us know we're walking a little bit differently and talking a little bit differently, and they're trying to figure out what it is.

You may know a thing or two about surrender. When you surrendered, God increased you on the down-low. When you surrendered, God said, "Now I can pour more trust in you. Now I can pour more faith in you. Now I can give you more of My spirit."

Maybe you're looking for financial increase. I'm here to let you know that the increase God has done inside you is better than any dollar amount you could ever receive. You're stronger than you were before. You believe God in a way you never did before. That heartbreak was increase in disguise. That betrayal was increase in disguise. You didn't know it, but it pushed you closer to God. You didn't know it, but it made you start crying out to God in a way you never cried out before.

When the angel of the Lord came to Mary and said, "Rejoice, highly favored one . . . blessed are you among women!" (Luke 1:28), Mary was afraid because she didn't realize this was increase in disguise. Sometimes God visits you, and what makes you afraid is actually increase in disguise. I don't know what you're up against right now, but I want you to understand that it is actually developing you. I know you're weary, but I want you to understand that every obstacle is an opportunity for increase.

God would not allow something to be taken from you if He didn't know how to multiply you in such a way that what was taken from you changes who you are on the inside.

Increase in disguise will have you looking at a shepherd boy with a lunch box, thinking he could not possibly run up on Goliath, telling him he should go back to the field and let the big, strong, bold people take care of the giant (1 Samuel 17:17–33). They said David wasn't enough. God said this was increase in disguise.

You may look at your situation and think, *Lord, this is not enough*, but God says, "This is increase in disguise." Don't expect people to see what God sees. David had more courage inside him than the giant had muscle. David was increase in disguise.

I want you to start looking at what you have to work with and recognize where you may be saying it's not enough, but God is saying, "I'll take whatever you have because whatever you have is something I can use. It's increase in disguise."

## LAY IT DOWN

I'm going to lay it all down because when I give it to God, He brings about increase.

## 61 Best-Laid Plans

Though He slay me, yet will I trust Him.

JOB 13:15

**YOU MAY BE FAMILIAR WITH THE STORY OF THE DEATH OF** Lazarus in John 11. Now, when Lazarus died, his sisters, Martha and Mary, thought, *We're in trouble, but we have a friend who can get us out of trouble.* They sent word to Jesus, but He didn't respond—and because He didn't respond, not only were Martha and Mary dealing with the grief of losing their brother, but they were also dealing with the feeling that their connection with Jesus was not as strong as they thought it was.

When Jesus finally began to head to where they were, Martha met Him on the way, but Mary stayed in the house. Martha said to Jesus, "Lord, if You had been here, my brother would not have died. But even now I know that whatever You ask of God, God will give You" (vv. 21–22).

She wasn't saying, "Okay, Jesus, now You can bring my brother back to life." What she was saying was, "I'm trying to make sense of this reality that You had the power but didn't use it. I know that whatever we ask of God He'll do, so I'm trying to figure out why You didn't respond to the thing I need."

Let's look at what happened next:

Jesus said to her, "Your brother will rise again."
  Martha said to Him, "I know that he will rise again in the resurrection at the last day. "
  Jesus said to her, "I am the resurrection and the life. He who believes in Me, though he may die, he shall live. And whoever lives and believes in Me shall never die. Do you believe this?"

She said to Him, "Yes, Lord, I believe that You are the Christ, the Son of God, who is to come into the world." (vv. 23–27)

Something happens when we begin to recognize that it's possible to move from one stage to another and never realize it. Sometimes we decline and don't even notice. There have been times when I looked at my life and realized I was so far off track that I couldn't even retrace my steps. I didn't notice that I was walking by sight and no longer by faith. I had declined. I'd been so busy having my purpose, my vision, and my talent come to life that I didn't realize I had taken ownership of something that started with God.

What happened? When did I start declining? Maybe I should have rested when somebody said they would help me. Maybe I should have asked for help. Maybe I should have asked somebody to give me some wisdom instead of trying to be Superwoman.

When I meet Martha in this text, she is declining. Most people would look at this text and say, "Well, she's lost her brother. Of course she's declining." But Martha wasn't just grieving the loss of a person. She was grieving the loss of her plan. Martha had a plan she felt should have saved her from being in this situation.

Have you ever tried to intervene in your own situation and your plan didn't work? You did all the things you knew to do, but your plan still did not work. When we grieve something, we're not just grieving what we lost; we're grieving what we believed could have been. We're grieving what will never be again.

## LAY IT DOWN

Even when my plan doesn't work, I know God is with me.

## 62 The Issue with Surrender

He heals the brokenhearted and binds up their wounds.

PSALM 147:3

**GRIEF—THAT IS THE ISSUE WITH SURRENDER. I WISH** surrender was easy. It's only easy when you're on the other side of it, but when it's time for you to lay something down, that surrender is grief.

When we find Jesus in the garden of Gethsemane in Luke 22 and get to those famous words—"Nevertheless not My will, but Yours, be done" (v. 42)—we act like that was the final part of what He said, but it's not. Verse 44 says, "And being in agony, He prayed more earnestly." Yes, He said those words, but He said them from a place of agony. If you are waiting for surrender to be easy, you will never lay it all down. You have to be willing to grieve the thing that must be surrendered.

People sometimes ask why you can't just get over something. In order for you to get over it, you have to create a memorial service for that thing. You've got to make preparations to lay that thing down. You don't just come into a space and lay down something that you thought would save your life, something that you thought would be your destiny, something that you thought would make the difference in your life. It takes a certain level of grief.

When Martha told Jesus, "If You had been here, my brother would not have died" (John 11:21), what I hear Martha saying is, "If You really cared about me, You would have responded to the thing I asked You to do." Martha didn't realize that she wanted to know if God cared about her.

But what Jesus wanted to show her was this: "Martha, I didn't come when you wanted Me to because I had a plan that was bigger than you could have imagined. But I came right here, right now, because I care for you in such a way that makes you realize I still see you, that makes you realize I still have a plan."

Jesus was saying to Martha, "I want to care for that broken heart. I want to care for that disappointment. I want to care for that discouragement. I'm coming to get that grief. I'm coming to get that disappointment. I'm coming to rectify the situation. I didn't intervene when you wanted Me to, but I did not ignore you altogether, because I care for you. I care so much for you that I took the time to have an exchange with you."

Jesus did not have to tell Martha anything. He could have walked right past her and gone straight to the tomb and brought Lazarus back to life. But because He cared so much for Martha, He took the time to hear her disappointment. And He cares enough to take the time to hear your discouragement too.

There have been some moments when I wondered if God was going to be good to me or when I felt like He forgot me. I learned after the fact that He didn't leave me or forsake me (Hebrews 13:5), but in the moment I felt like He wasn't going to show up.

Maybe you're saying, "God, if You had been there, I would have never been touched." "God, if You had been there, I would have never gone through that divorce." "God, if You had been there, I would have never gone through that betrayal."

God is saying to you, "You can go through this because by the time I get finished taking care of you, you'll have no question about whether or not I care about you."

## LAY IT DOWN

I serve a God who will go out of His way to make sure I am seen because He cares for me.

## 63 Fresh Faith

Lord, I believe; help my unbelief!

MARK 9:24

**WHEN WE SEE MARTHA HAVING HER EXCHANGE WITH** Jesus in John 11, Jesus was revealing to her, "I didn't come when you needed Me to, but I have a plan in the midst of everything that's happening." What I love about this is Jesus didn't try to convince Martha to not grieve the death of her brother, Lazarus. Jesus didn't tell her to just get over it. Jesus started asking her questions about what she believed.

This is important because in moments when grief will not let go of you, the only thing you may be able to do is grieve and believe at the same time. Jesus didn't strip Martha of her grief. He was saying, "You can keep your grief. I want to know what you believe, because if you can grieve and believe at the same time, then your belief will overwhelm your grief."

When Jesus was talking to Martha, He needed her to believe on a different level. God needed Martha to believe something about God that she never had before. When He asked Martha, "Do you believe this?" (v. 26), Martha started repeating a Pharisee-like belief: "Yes, I believe in the last days that he's going to come back."

But Jesus was saying to her, "No, you're going to have to believe something about God that you have never believed before."

This is not a season for recycled belief. If you are going to break out of your grief or out of your situation, you are going to have to believe something about God that you have never had to believe before: "God, I wanted You to be here, but if You didn't show up, maybe You are increasing my belief. I'm going to have to believe that my destiny is not ruined and that You can heal me and restore me. I've got to believe that You'll get me through, that You'll give me wisdom and strategy. I've got to believe something about You that I've never had to believe before."

You're not going to get the job done with recycled belief, so put down your grandmother's faith. This ain't a job for your mother's faith or your pastor's faith. This is a job for new faith. You're going to have to believe that the debt is already paid, that you are never forsaken, that you may be alone but you're never lonely, that there are angels watching over you. You're going to have to believe on a different level.

If you're going to have breakthrough in your life, it's not going to happen because you stayed seated in your grief. Say, "God, I'm grieving, but I'm also believing that I've got a shot and that my best days are ahead of me. I'm not saying it didn't hurt; I'm just saying I'm believing something about You, God, that I've never had to believe before."

That's why that old, recycled belief isn't working. That's why those same old prayers don't have the power they once had. That's your old, recycled belief. It worked for you back then, but you're going to have to surrender what you used to believe to lay hold of this new belief.

## LAY IT DOWN

With God's help, I'm going to believe something about God I've never had to believe before.

## 64 Grieve, Then Believe

God blesses those who mourn, for they will be comforted.
MATTHEW 5:4 NLT

**IN JOHN 11, JESUS SAID SOMETHING TO MARTHA THAT HE** didn't say very often in Scripture. In a moment when Martha was struggling to believe, He said to her, "I'm going to show you something about Me that nobody else sees." In the moment of her greatest disbelief, He gave her a revelation that even the most faithful didn't get to hold. He said, "I am the resurrection and the life" (John 11:25).

Jesus didn't go around talking about who He was; He just embodied who He was. But because this woman was struggling so much, He said to Martha, "Come here close to Me. I'm going to tell you who I am."

Something about John 11 stood out to me and helped me to understand that the first step of surrender is not laying it all down—it's grieving, then believing, then laying it all down. I found it fascinating that when Martha had this moment with Jesus, the text tells us she said, "Lord, I believe that you are the Christ," but we can tell there's still a little dissonance in her belief (John 11:27).

It says she went to tell Mary, her sister, "The Teacher has come and is calling for you" (v. 28). So I went and read the chapter again to see when Jesus called for her, but Jesus never said, "Go get Mary." It's almost as if when Martha couldn't believe it on her own that she had to go find a woman who could believe on a level that she couldn't. Martha needed a sister to hear what Jesus had said because she was struggling to believe it on her own, but if she got a sister who could believe what God said, maybe her sister could help her make sense of what was happening in her life.

When Martha went to get Mary, she did not just get any ordinary woman. She went to get a woman who would know how to pour out her oil on His feet and wash them with her hair (John 12:3). She went and got a woman who understood that "I don't always understand His plans, but I trust who He is." I don't know if you are Martha or Mary, but I know you've got to be one or the other. No woman should be untouched reading this book because you and I are about to believe God on a level we've never had to believe before.

My friend, God is saying to you, "I want to give you something that you would have never had otherwise." I need you to believe God for healing not just in your body but in the area you've had to surrender. I need you to believe Jesus not only cares *about* you but cares *for* you. He's saying, "I care so much for you that I protected you. I care so much for you that I kept you here. I care so much for you that I sent that grandmother. I sent that teacher. You keep giving Me a list of all the things that make you feel like I don't care about you, but you're missing all the ways that I did care for you. And I care for you now."

## LAY IT DOWN

No matter what I have been through, I've never been out of God's care.

## 65 Worth the Grief

> The LORD is close to the brokenhearted and saves those who are crushed in spirit.
>
> PSALM 34:18 NIV

**IN JOHN 11, AFTER HER BROTHER, LAZARUS, DIED,** Martha was trying to figure out why Jesus hadn't come to help earlier, probably saying to herself, *I thought we were friends and I know You cared then, but do You care now?*

Being in relationship with Jesus doesn't mean He always responds in the way we anticipate. That's frustrating because we have an idea of what care looks like and then we have to surrender our definition. You're thinking, *God if You really cared about me . . .*

But God says to you, "I care for you, but Me caring for you doesn't always mean you get the things you want. What it does mean is I am going to show you that I couldn't give you what you wanted when you wanted it, but what I had for you was worth the wait."

What God has for you is going to be worth the grief. What God has for you is going to be worth every tear you have shed. It's going to be worth every heartbreak you've ever had.

My prayer for you is that you won't miss the moment of increase because increase is often disguised. Sometimes it looks like heartbreak. Sometimes it looks like loss. But if we are expecting response only in one area, we may miss the increase available to us in other areas. So my question to you is, What do you need to grieve? And what is it that you need to believe?

Maybe you don't have to work twice as hard. Maybe you need to let that person go. Maybe you need to forgive and let that situation hurt you because sometimes you're so tough you won't admit that it hurts, but maybe grieving for you is admitting that it hurts. Don't let the Enemy get you stuck in grief. You can grieve and believe at the same time.

I believe you're healed. I believe that God's going to walk you through it. I believe that He's going to protect you and preserve you. I believe He's going to convict you and comfort you. I believe He's going to transform you. I believe He's going to call your people to you. I believe He's going to give you wisdom. I believe He's going to give you insight. I believe He's going to give you patience. I believe He's going to give you joy. I believe He will give beauty for ashes (Isaiah 61:3). I believe He will restore what the locust has eaten (Joel 2:25). I believe who He says He is. I believe He'll do what He says He will do. I believe He's still faithful. I know you're questioning, but I believe. I've seen Him do it.

I believe you haven't seen your best day yet. I believe rivers of living water are going to flow out of your room. Whom the Son has set free is free indeed (John 8:36), and I decree and declare everything that God put in you must come out. I demand it to come out.

I believe somebody's creativity is coming back. I demand it to come forth in the name of Jesus, in the name that is above every name (Philippians 2:9). I speak Jesus over your life. God's got a bird's-eye view of your life, and when you see what He sees, you're going to recognize that it was all working out in your favor. When it's all said and done, you're going to see it the way God sees it.

## LAY IT DOWN

What do I need to lay on the altar, and what does God want me to pick up?

## 66 These Dry Bones

Anyone who belongs to Christ has become a new person. The old life is gone; a new life has begun!

2 CORINTHIANS 5:17 NLT

**EZEKIEL WAS A PROPHET IN THE DAYS OF OLD TESTAMENT** Israel. The book of the Bible that bears his name tells about some spectacular visions he received from God. One day, Ezekiel was taken in the Spirit and dropped into a valley filled with dry bones. God asked him, "Can these bones live?" (Ezekiel 37:3). And he said, "O Lord God, You know" (v. 4). God then told Ezekiel to prophesy to the bones. He did as he was commanded. Suddenly, muscle and tissue and flesh covered the bones, but no breath was in them. They were what I would call the walking dead. They looked put together. They looked like they should have breath in them, but they didn't.

Traditionally, when I've heard anyone preach this text, they start from the moment where many dry bones are lying around. But when I was studying, God told me to start from the point where the bones are put together but don't have breath. Because so many of us are put together, but we just don't have any breath or we're down to our last breath. We don't start holding our breath because we have plenty of it. We're holding our breath because it's the only thing keeping us together.

Ezekiel said:

> So I prophesied as I was commanded; and as I prophesied, there was a noise, and suddenly a rattling; and the bones came together, bone to bone. Indeed, as I looked, the sinews and the flesh came upon them, and the skin covered them over; but there was no breath in them.

Also He said to me, "Prophesy to the breath, prophesy, son of man, and say to the breath, 'Thus says the Lord God: "Come from the four winds, O breath, and breathe on these slain, that they may live."'" So I prophesied as He commanded me, and breath came into them, and they lived, and stood upon their feet, an exceedingly great army.

Then He said to me, "Son of man, these bones are the whole house of Israel. They indeed say, 'Our bones are dry, our hope is lost, and we ourselves are cut off!' Therefore prophesy and say to them, 'Thus says the Lord God: "Behold, O My people, I will open your graves and cause you to come up from your graves, and bring you into the land of Israel. Then you shall know that I am the Lord, when I have opened your graves, O My people, and brought you up from your graves. I will put My Spirit in you, and you shall live, and I will place you in your own land."'" (37:7–14)

Just like God said to Ezekiel, He is saying to you today, "I've got territory set aside just for you. You're not just going to live, but I'm going to position you. It's one thing to live, but you're not going to live lost. I'm going to take you into your own land, and then you shall know that I, the Lord, have spoken it and performed it. I'm not just a God who speaks. I'll perform. I can back up anything I say."

## LAY IT DOWN

What has been dry and dead in my life, God wants to resurrect.

# 67 This World Is Not My Home

Your eyes saw my unformed body; all the days ordained for me were written in your book before one of them came to be.

PSALM 139:16 NIV

**WHEN A PERSON IS EXILED, THEY HAVE BEEN EXPELLED** and barred from their native country. The thing about being exiled is that if you've been exiled long enough, you'll forget what your life was like before you began living in a foreign land.

You may have been exiled away from your native land. I'm not talking about your ethnicity. I'm talking about being exiled to the foreign land of grief, depression, worry, doubt. And sometimes it starts off foreign, but eventually it becomes your norm. You're just kind of used to walking around broken. You're used to walking around with no expectations anymore.

If you've been exiled long enough, you'll start to give up on what life was like before you got barred from joy, from peace, from hope, from confidence. Some circumstances in your life are so devastating you feel exiled.

In Ezekiel's vision of the dry bones in Ezekiel 37, the children of Israel had been exiled from their homeland. And spiritually, they were beginning to take on the characteristics of the foreign land they were living in. They were hopeless. Their bones were dry. They felt cut off. And they had forgotten that their spirit had a native country.

In Jeremiah 1:5, God said, "Before I formed you in the womb I knew you." You lived somewhere else before you were formed in your mother's womb. Technically, your mother's womb was foreign to you because before God placed you in your mother's womb, you were somewhere else.

Before you were born, God knew you. He knew you in the spiritual realm. He understood and connected with you on a level that humanity can't. Picking back up in Jeremiah 1:5, God said, "Before you were born I sanctified you; I ordained you a prophet to the nations."

I want you to know that even though you are no longer tapped into heaven the way you were before you were formed in your mother's womb, you still have access to that native country. You did not start in the place where you've been exiled; you started in a place that you cannot see.

Heaven knew exactly where you were going to be in this season of your life because before you came here, heaven laid out the road map. Heaven gave you enough spirit and strength for the life ahead of you. Heaven knew you. Heaven is saying your name.

We're trying to get back to our native land. We're trying to step over our situation and step back to the place where heaven formed us. We're trying to reconnect to holiness. We're trying to reconnect to who we were before we touched down here because who we were there had enough power for here.

## LAY IT DOWN

Heaven has a house with my name on it.

## 68 Made Holy

> You were washed, you were sanctified, you were justified in the name of the Lord Jesus Christ and by the Spirit of our God.
>
> 1 CORINTHIANS 6:11 NIV

**DON'T FORGET WHERE YOU CAME FROM. YOU ARE NOT OF** this earth. You are a daughter of the Most High God. Before God formed you in your mother's womb, He knew you (Jeremiah 1:5). God didn't half make you. He didn't give you just a little bit to work with. He said, "I'm going to give her everything she needs for the road ahead of her." You may not understand, but that's all right.

You feel like you're running out of breath. God says to you, "That's impossible. Because before I formed you in your mother's womb, I put enough breath in you for the life ahead of you."

You think you're running out of strength. God says to you, "That's impossible. Because before I formed you in your mother's womb, I knew you. And I didn't put you on this earth with just enough to get you halfway there. Do you think you came all this way to do some half-stepping? If you're going to step in this world, you're going to step in it with all of heaven's resources backing you up. You are not running out of breath."

As a matter of fact, you're about to dig deeper. I hear God saying, "You've got to exhale." Because when you exhale, you can inhale. See, you're holding on to that breath. God says to you, "I wish you would let it go. I wish you would just cry the ugly cry. I wish you would just say that you're broken. I wish you would just say that you're worried. Because if you would finally let that thing go, I can show you what else I put in you."

You think we serve a God of one breath? God said, "I will . . .

multiply thee" (Genesis 17:2 KJV). He's not just multiplying your money. He's not just multiplying your friends. He's multiplying your breath.

If you're bold, I dare you to take a breath. If you take a breath, heaven says, "I'm going to show you that you've got more in you than you think. I'm going to show you what I knew when I formed you in your mother's womb. I made you holy. You are not a broken little girl. You are not unlovable. You are not someone who can be held down. I was holding you before your mother ever held you."

We've got to get back to glory. We are focused on what's happening here, but God is focused on what's happening there. We are not of this world. We didn't start here. We started with God.

You didn't start here. You started with God. Your life did not begin when the divorce happened. Your life did not begin when the abortion occurred. Your life did not begin when the addiction happened. Nor did it end. Those don't have anything to do with who God is. God says, "I'm holy enough to be with you when you're in addiction, and I'm holy enough to be with you when you're in ministry. And if you get a revelation of My holiness, then you'll start tapping into holiness and get out of your feelings, out of your past, out of your emotions, and you'll step into My holiness. You'll say, "God, I want to be sanctified again. God, can You make me holy again? Remove anything in me that's making me dirty."

God doesn't care how dirty you've been. He can still sanctify you because He's just that holy.

## LAY IT DOWN

I don't have to worry about what will happen if things don't go the way I want them to. God is holy enough to see me through whatever I'm up against.

## 69 Remember God's Holiness

I do not do this for your sake, O house of Israel, but for My holy name's sake, which you have profaned among the nations wherever you went. And I will sanctify My great name . . . and the nations shall know that I am the Lord.

EZEKIEL 36:22–23

**IF THE ENEMY CAN GET YOU TO QUESTION GOD'S INTEN**-tions, then you will question the holiness of God. And you'll think that God is trying to keep something from you. But when you have a revelation about God's holiness, you'll know that if God is keeping something from you, then it must be something that could harm you. It must not mean well by you.

In Ezekiel 36:22, God said to Israel, "I do not do this for your sake, O house of Israel, but for My holy name's sake, which you have profaned among the nations wherever you went." He was saying, "My holiness is on the line."

You may think it's about your circumstance; you think it's about your situation. But the truth is, you're questioning God's holiness. You're saying, "God, if I'm honest, I don't know if You know what You're doing, because if You knew what You were doing, why would You allow this pain, this grief, this disease?"

So you took your breath back, you took your worship back, you took your trust back, and you took your faith back because you lost faith in God's holiness. You said, "God, how can my marriage be in trouble? I'm gonna take my faith back. I'm gonna hold on to it because when I gave it to You, You disappointed me. When I gave it to You, it didn't go the way I thought it should. So I'm just going to take it back."

When we find Israel in the text, they had started serving other gods. They probably didn't know it fully because they probably still had God somewhere in the mix, but they had started serving other gods because you don't just take your trust back from God; you place it in something else. You say, "I took my trust from God; now I'm going to trust my brokenness because my brokenness says I can't trust God."

It's not like you just move your faith away from God; you switch it to another pot. You say, "Now I'm going to have faith in my own decisions. I'm going to have faith in my own plans. I'm going to have faith in other people. I'm going to have faith that someone else will fix me because when I gave it to God, He didn't perform the way I thought He should perform."

## LAY IT DOWN

God is holy, so if He's keeping something from me, then it must be something that could harm me. I give my faith back to God.

## 70  Buried Alive

> Then you shall know that I am the Lord, when I have opened your graves, O My people, and brought you up from your graves.
>
> EZEKIEL 37:13

**IN EZEKIEL 37, ISRAEL HAD SPENT SEVENTY YEARS** exiled from the land God gave them. Because they had spent seventy years in a foreign place, exiled from their homeland, they were in a dilemma: They were buried alive.

Have you been buried alive? This is what happens to us when we find ourselves in predicaments where we are alive, but we feel buried by what has exiled us. We're buried in uncertainty. I wouldn't even call it depression. I wouldn't call it grief; we're just buried, and we don't even know why we're here. And we can't see beyond that any longer.

In the text, Israel was buried alive. They said, "Our bones are dry, our hope is lost, and we ourselves are cut off!" (v. 11). These are three signs that you're buried alive, that you're down to your last breath.

Number one, your bones are dry. You may be saying, "Sis, I put on lotion. I don't know what you're talking about. You lost me. These bones are not dry. I put on Vaseline, just like my grandmother told me." But that word *bones* in Ezekiel 37 means "substance." You don't have substance anymore. Faith is the substance of things hoped for, and your substance has run dry. When your bones are dry, it means you don't know what you're made of anymore. You don't even know who you are anymore. That's what it feels like when your bones are dry. Your substance has dried up.

Number two, your hope is lost. I love that the text says their hope was lost. It doesn't say their hope was gone. Because hope being lost means we can have it one day, but we don't have it the next. That word *lost* literally means wandering.

Number three, you are cut off. That means that where you were once standing tall, you are now cut off. Maybe it's in your career. Maybe it's in your relationship. Maybe it's your faith that feels cut off. You experienced church hurt. You weren't able to get over why God didn't deliver you the way you thought He would. And so you have been cut off.

This is where Israel was in the text. Their bones were dry, their hope was lost, and they had been cut off.

So God said to the prophet Ezekiel, "I have an assignment that's going to bring them back to life." Notice that when God was ready to restore Israel, He gave a prophet a vision. While Israel felt cut off and like they had no hope, there was a prophet who saw them alive. So you have to understand what's happening behind the scenes of the text.

Behind the scenes of the text, Israel was down to their last breath. But on the other side of the text, God was giving them a word, saying, "Exhale. I want you to come to a place where you feel like you're out of breath. But in the moment that I begin speaking, breath is going to come back to you."

## LAY IT DOWN

When I feel like I'm down to my last breath, God can breathe life back into me.

## 71 Conflicted but Still Listening

> The woman said to Him, "I know that Messiah is coming" (who is called Christ). "When He comes, He will tell us all things." Jesus said to her, "I who speak to you am He."
>
> JOHN 4:25–26

**WHEN WE HAVE ELECTIONS, BOTH SIDES OF THE AISLE** work overtime to assure us they have a foolproof plan to lead the American people. For many of us, we look forward to the end of the political ads that run during every TV break. It is interesting for me, at least, to watch candidates debate about important issues. Even when I don't agree with what is being said, I listen. There is something to be said about being conflicted but still listening.

That's where we find the woman at the well when she was talking to Jesus in John 4. Their encounter is layered with conflict. At the time, it was not socially acceptable for Jews and Samaritans to comingle. Even the disciples were surprised by Jesus talking to her. The Samaritan woman, according to their customs, should not have been at the well during that time of day, and she certainly should not have been talking to a Jewish man. As we know, and she was soon to find out, Jesus wasn't just any man. He was the Messiah.

By cultural standards, this woman didn't have the best reputation. She had been married five times and had a connection with a sixth man, as Jesus prophetically pointed out. So imagine how seen and valued she probably felt in this moment, talking to a man who wasn't a potential suitor. I'm imagining that she was able to be herself—no false pretenses, able to let her guard down.

Society had deemed her an outcast, but in their uncommon

encounter, Jesus favored her. This moment at the well shows us that Jesus desires unity, having no interest in being divisive or subscribing to the laws of man.

Have you ever been like the woman at the well? In conflict with accepting the status quo but hearing God call you higher?

By man's standards, it doesn't add up that God would use someone like me, a divorced teen mom who dropped out of college to preach the gospel to millions of women—conflicted but still listening. It doesn't make sense that He would use a virgin to give birth to our Savior—conflicted but still listening. Who God has ordained for you to become may never make sense to man, but it has to make sense to you. You can be conflicted, but you must listen to His voice.

Though conflicted, the woman at the well listened, and she didn't gatekeep Jesus' presence for herself. She went back to the very people in her community who saw her as an outcast, and she told them about her encounter with Jesus. I'm sure they were conflicted to hear about Jesus from her, but they listened.

There may be conflict in the place you're most familiar with—maybe it's within your family or your work environment—but there's also some familiarity about Jesus that you can share in the midst of the conflict. Allow yourself to live a life surrendered to listening to God's voice. Walk by faith and not by sight. Stand in unity with other women, especially those whom society has perpetually claimed you have nothing in common with. And when someone asks how you're able to be so graceful in the midst of conflict, I hope you'll tell them that you can still hear Jesus through all the noise.

## LAY IT DOWN

Even when I feel conflicted, I can still listen and hear Jesus through all the noise.

## 72 Cemented by Maybe

> Jonathan said to the young man who bore his armor, "Come, let us go over to the garrison of these uncircumcised; it may be that the Lord will work for us. For nothing restrains the Lord from saving by many or by few."
>
> 1 SAMUEL 14:6

**HAVE YOU EVER BEEN IN A HEALING SEASON OF YOUR LIFE** and a situation arises that threatens that process? How do you handle those demands? Maybe it's the opportunity to fall in love again after an unexpected heartbreak. Or maybe it's the possibility to expand your family after experiencing a miscarriage or an unsuccessful adoption. Does the situation make you want to hide or trust that God will pull you through it if you have to endure another heartbreak?

We can see an example of this choice in 1 Samuel 14, where Jonathan was leading Israel against an army. If Jonathan had taken on the attitude of the people he was with, he would have cowered in fear at the great contrast of Israel's army compared to the Philistines. They were outnumbered and ill-equipped for the battle ahead of them, but Jonathan knew that if the Lord was on their side, the comparison didn't matter. He may not have been completely sure, but he didn't allow his uncertainty to automatically disqualify him or to diminish his faith. Jonathan moved on a maybe because he trusted God.

*What if I trust God's track record of doing the impossible?* is what I imagine Jonathan thinking as he led his armor-bearer into a battle against the Philistines. For us, before backing down from obstacles, maybe we should begin asking ourselves this question: *Have I even considered what God may be able to do?*

Surrendering to moving in uncertainty doesn't equate to an automatic win, and that's okay. God isn't a genie in a bottle who grants every wish we have. He realizes that if we received our definition of winning in every season, then we wouldn't need faith, and we certainly wouldn't need to be in relationship with Him.

Surrendering to maybe is how you strengthen your faith muscle for the journey ahead of you. You might not have the whole plan, but you know that you have a word from God. The obedience of moving in the direction of where God has called you might have to be cemented by a maybe. That's when God knows He can trust you with more of the plan, because you were willing to take a step of faith based on a maybe.

You'll know God is partnering with you in the realm of a maybe because He will send you glimpses of His presence along the way. Listen for His voice. Watch for His hand. Be still enough to catch the wind of His flow. Suddenly, you'll retire from leaning on your own understanding and start dwelling in a level of peace that surpasses all understanding (Proverbs 3:5; Philippians 4:7).

Jonathan refused to accept that this situation was the end. He took a chance on what God might want to do.

Your situation may look like it's the end, but maybe it's the beginning of something beautiful.

You've let your mind play the game of maybe, assessing all the ways things could go wrong. Now you need to let your spirit start wondering what God could do in the situation you're worried about. Let your spirit start running wild in the direction of maybe. See how good it can get when God partners with you.

## LAY IT DOWN

I'm willing to trust God's maybe and think about the best that could happen in my situation.

## 73 Claim Your Holy Identity

The Lord spoke to Moses, saying, "Take the rod; you and your brother Aaron gather the congregation together. Speak to the rock before their eyes, and it will yield its water; thus you shall bring water for them out of the rock, and give drink to the congregation and their animals."

NUMBERS 20:7–8

**HAS GOD EVER CALLED YOU TO DO SOMETHING THAT YOU** thought was so out of your league it would take a miracle for you to accomplish it? Something that made your heart beat a little bit faster, and the mere thought of it made your mind race with endless possibilities of how you could mess it up?

Maybe it wasn't even something that was unfamiliar to you. In fact, you'd been praying for it to come to fruition—such as pitching an idea to a brand you want to work with, or writing a book or song that this generation needs. But you dismissed your trust in God and deviated from the faith that led you to be standing in the middle of your answered prayer. You decided to trust your own logic—subscribing to imposter syndrome or discrediting your God-given abilities—instead of trusting the possibility of God equipping you to carry out His plan.

In Numbers 20:8, God gave Moses clear instructions for how to break open the rock to quench the thirst of the children of Israel and their animals: "Speak to the rock . . . and it will yield its water." Yet Moses did what made him comfortable. He trusted his own logic more than God's holiness. I've done this before too. I've seen what I was up against and thought I had accounted for all the resources readily available to me. There were times when I didn't consider the power of heaven's resources that were backing me up.

If we believe we're made in the image of God, as it says in Genesis 1:27, then why is it difficult for us to live in the consciousness of being surrendered to God's holiness?

What does it mean for you to be surrendered to God's holiness? It means accepting the fact that you are set apart to be God's chosen solution to an issue. Your pathway to holiness is remaining close to God, learning His character through His Word.

When God starts speaking to you in miracle form, giving you a plan that seems beyond human logic, it should begin to pique your curiosity for how He sees you. It should become your sign that you are set apart. Too often, when God starts giving us a plan that requires us to be unconventional, either we brush it off or get scared and then wonder why we can't seem to get to the other side of our Red Sea.

When you trust that you're set apart, you'll also trust that there's grace for you to be and do whatever God has called you to.

Your internal self-talk will begin to reflect how God speaks to you. It will become second nature for your decisions to be influenced by the Holy Spirit. You'll become more diligent about learning your triggers and how to abandon trauma responses that have kept you from relying on God.

When you settle into your set-apart era, you will find yourself seriously considering that God knows something about you that you can't fully comprehend. It may make you nervous, but it will also make you hungry for more of His presence. Are you ready to surrender to your holy identity?

## LAY IT DOWN

I'm ready to claim my holy identity as set apart by God to do whatever He has called me to do.

## 74 *The Power to Pivot*

> Listen, all you of Judah and you inhabitants of Jerusalem, and you, King Jehoshaphat! Thus says the Lord to you: "Do not be afraid nor dismayed because of this great multitude, for the battle is not yours, but God's."
>
> 2 CHRONICLES 20:15

**HAVE YOU EVER BEEN FACE-TO-FACE WITH SOMETHING** that could quite literally take you out? Not just something that could knock the wind out of your sails, but something that's trying to take away the very breath that God has so graciously given you? It didn't start out that way though. It was a blessing . . . until it wasn't. One day you looked up, and it had become a heavy burden that your shoulders weren't strong enough to carry.

In one season it felt like you were powerful when you relied on yourself to fight your battles. That was survival mode, and you mastered it. In another season, however, that mindset of survival became a surefire pathway toward self-destruction. The tools and mindset you need to survive can't be your only sources of strength. You get to decide which season you're in—survival or surrender.

In 2 Chronicles 20, King Jehoshaphat of Judah was leading his people when he found out that the military alliance of the Moabites, Ammonites, and others was on its way to attack the people of Judah. Imagine that you're Jehoshaphat, and you realize that your enemies want to go beyond resetting your plan. Your enemies want nothing more than to snatch your life from the earth and every bit of life that's connected to you.

Maybe you don't have to imagine this because you've either been in this position before or you're standing in it right now.

The Enemy is attempting to hijack the vision God gave you that generations would benefit from. You get to decide whether you're going to continue to try to survive the attacks of the Enemy based on your own wisdom or if you'll trust God to fight on your behalf.

Jehoshaphat didn't choose to merely survive the attack that he knew was coming. He chose to depend on something greater than an army of men he could assemble. He consulted with God about how to handle his enemies.

We can't keep living life in survival mode. It's doing us no good, and it's got us believing that trusting God is a part-time thing. Stop treating God like a secret lover. Whether you've been someone who creates rigid boundaries, shuts down when it's time to talk through an uncomfortable situation, or has trust issues because holding on to grudges seems safer than communicating that betrayal actually hurts, it's time to hand it all over to God and ask Him for the power to pivot away from survivalist behavior.

Power isn't a monolith. It is fluid. There are times when power will cause you to move. Other times power will declare for you to stand still, just as God told Jehoshaphat in 2 Chronicles 20:17 and the children of Israel as they were escaping the Egyptians (Exodus 14:13). God took ownership of the battle that Jehoshaphat was preparing to face.

Jehoshaphat did as he was told, and God protected him and the people of Judah. Now imagine how free Jehoshaphat must have felt knowing that God is a promise keeper! I hope this encourages you to trust God with every battle that comes your way. There's freedom in the midst of every battle that God is fighting on your behalf.

## LAY IT DOWN

It's time for me to hand my burden to God and ask Him for the power to pivot away from survivalist behavior.

## 75 Silent Transition of Power

The Lord said to Moses, "Why do you cry to Me? Tell the children of Israel to go forward."

EXODUS 14:15

**WHEN WE MEET THE CHILDREN OF ISRAEL IN EXODUS 14,** their distrust of the plan God gave to Moses was on full display. They questioned Moses' motives and were a heartbeat away from turning their backs on freedom to return to being enslaved by the Egyptians.

As God had instructed him, Moses told the people to trust God's promise to deliver them from their enemy and into Canaan, the land of freedom that God had prepared for them.

I don't know what represents Egypt in your life—maybe it's a toxic relationship or work environment—but I dare you to believe what Moses told the children of Israel in verse 14: "The Lord will fight for you, and you shall hold your peace."

For the Israelites, and maybe for you as well, accepting the truth that God will show up can sometimes be just as difficult as leaving a familiar environment, even one that is bursting at the seams with oppression.

The children of Israel had to trust God in a way that they'd never done before. They had to trust that God would protect them again. Trusting God to perform another miracle can sometimes feel like we're asking for too much, especially when we've been oppressed or given the bare minimum for too long. Can you relate?

I've had to trust God with my ministry, Woman Evolve. As it's grown, I've had to deepen my trust in God's plan for it and for me. I've had to trust that His power, wisdom, and creativity will never run out. So even when it feels like I'm running low on creativity, wisdom, or resources to create environments for us to be in His presence together, I trust that the power that started this thing will meet me when I need it the most—which is every single moment!

An exchange of power happens in this text, and if we're not careful, we'll miss it. There's a silent transition of power between Moses and God. When Moses went to God and shared a vulnerable moment, God said to him, "Why do you cry to Me?" (v. 15) before He gave him instructions on how to overcome the Egyptians.

If you think back over your life, I'm sure you can find a few silent transitions of power. They're not always big, breathtaking moments that knock the wind out of us.

Sometimes power looks like raw honesty in the presence of God. Moses didn't hide his desperate need for God to intervene, and God didn't turn His back on Moses for coming to Him with unfiltered passion. There are moments when it takes courage to be angry, overwhelmed, vulnerable, and fragile with God. Sometimes we want to be the strongest version of ourselves for others, and it begins to translate into how we show up in His presence, but God longs for our authenticity.

When power seeps from us, maybe in moments of confusion or despair, we tend to pull away from God. In those moments, it's critical to remember this: Power left us, but it didn't leave God. Go back to Him and ask Him to refuel you for the journey ahead.

God equipped Moses with a plan, confidence, and power. He restored Moses' spirit just as He does for us.

## LAY IT DOWN

When I feel powerless, I will dare to ask God to give me His power for the journey ahead.

## 76 Intersection of Lost and Found

"Why were you searching for me?" he asked. "Didn't you know I had to be in my Father's house?" But they did not understand what he was saying to them.

LUKE 2:49–50 NIV

**AS WE READ THE BIBLE, WE SEE THAT THE PEOPLE GOD** used the most were people who lived at the intersections of being humanly complicated and heavenly divine, just like you and me. This communicates to me that intersections are gateways to redemption and reconciliation.

Think about David. He was a king, musician, and warrior. These are the intersections that pointed to him being chosen by God. But we can't skip over and ignore the fact that he was also a liar and an adulterer. We have to acknowledge the intersections of his humanity that made David appear as if he didn't even know God.

I recognize that just because we're called and anointed, we can't deny that we have internal battles we're fighting too. That's why we have to stay connected to God. If we are to truly believe that His strength will be made perfect in our weakness, then we must be willing to acknowledge when our own strengths and weaknesses are in competition so that we can be yoked up with something stronger (2 Corinthians 12:9; Matthew 11:29).

In Luke 2, when Mary and Joseph thought they had lost young Jesus at the temple, they went back for Him. Before Mary became pregnant with Jesus, she knew who she was being trusted to carry, so it must have surprised Jesus when they came back for Him. It should have come as no surprise to her or Joseph when

Jesus told them that He was at an intersection, the crossroads of being their son and our Savior.

Jesus was at the intersection of being human and divine. Somebody has to be able to relate to the world in order to save the world. Somebody has to relate to teen moms to know what they need to thrive. Somebody has to admit they had no idea what it took to be a successful CEO so that a new business owner won't get discouraged.

Jesus became our gateway to salvation, redemption, and reconciliation.

It takes courage to own your intersections and be used as a gateway. It takes courage to go to therapy and change how your bloodline addresses uncomfortable conversations. It takes courage to trust God on a level that you've never had to trust Him before. It takes courage to double down on a vision that God gave you when no one else dares to believe.

You are a lot of things. We all are. Your lived experiences may have come with some scars, but they are gateways for you to be used by God. Trust me, I'm telling you something that I am living. I had no idea what God could do with my life, but I trusted that His way was better than my pride, silence, and shame.

Yes, you can be healed and still healing. Yes, you can be loved and still working through your triggers. Yes, you can be a CEO and still not have it all figured out. But, sis, what you can't do is deny the power you've found in God when you were lost at an intersection that you didn't think He could use.

## LAY IT DOWN

My life may have some scars, but they are gateways for me to be used by God.

## 77 Don't Look Back

> Paul said, "I am a Jew from Tarsus, in Cilicia, a citizen of no mean city; and I implore you, permit me to speak to the people."
>
> ACTS 21:39

**TRUTH IS, NOT EVERYONE WILL TRUST YOUR GROWTH.** Does that mean you're supposed to shrink back to being the person they've always known you to be? Well, let's look at the Bible and see what God's Word says about it.

When we find Paul in Acts 21, he was being falsely accused of bringing Gentiles into the Jewish temple. A little backstory on Paul: He was previously known as Saul, a man who had violently persecuted Christians because of their beliefs. Eventually, he converted to Christianity, became one of Jesus' disciples, and went on to preach the gospel everywhere he went. This accusation was an attempt to get Paul to stop sharing the gospel, but their plan didn't work. Paul wrote letters from his jail cell that shared the truth about Jesus and converted more people into Christianity.

Maybe they thought this lie would work because of Paul's past. God restored and redeemed Paul. Maybe there is a narrative about you that others can't seem to let go of. Guess what? Your anointing, your healing, and the ways in which you've evolved, sis, none of them is up for negotiation.

Two things can be true: You can have a past that isn't so pretty, and it can still be used for the glory of God. You can have a past that makes you cringe and still have a hope and a future.

When you go back to those environments that expected the least from you, it's not your job to prove them right or wrong.

That's up to God. It's on Him to use His power to move through you in a way that's undeniable.

And if we're honest, sometimes we are the ones who won't trust our growth. People don't believe me when I say that I get nervous about preaching or public speaking. It's not that I don't trust that God will show up; He always does. Sometimes I don't trust myself. I have to worship my way through my own "stinking thinking." I don't back down from wherever God calls me to show up. I stand up to it because I've seen with my own eyes how God has used His power through me to help heal other women.

What is it about your past that has caused you to shy away from who God knows you to be? The story we rehearse is the story we end up releasing into the world. Maybe you failed at something in the past, but if you keep telling yourself that you're a failure, then you'll disguise it as being a perfectionist or a procrastinator who's waiting for the perfect moment to release what God gave her. When in reality, you're afraid to fail again.

You've got something no one else has, but it's up to you to believe it and not let your past deny you from releasing it.

## LAY IT DOWN

No matter what is in my past, I still have a hope and a future.

## 78 Make the Investment

Assuredly, I say to you, wherever this gospel is preached in the whole world, what this woman has done will also be told as a memorial to her.

MATTHEW 26:13

**HAVING THE DISCERNMENT TO KNOW WHEN TO INVEST** and when to save not only applies to our finances, but it also applies to how we honor our spiritual well-being. There are times when it's worth it to pour out what we've stored up, and there are times when we need to hold on to our harvest.

In Matthew 26, the woman poured an expensive oil on Jesus in preparation for His burial. The disciples questioned why she poured it out instead of selling it and giving the proceeds to the poor. Jesus corrected them, explaining that the poor would always be with them but He wouldn't and that this act of sacrifice toward Him would make this woman unforgettable.

This is surrender. This woman is one of our examples of being willing to lay down something of consequence. Otherwise, we're living life on the surface. Sure, she could have saved it for herself or sold it to make a profit, but she decided to do something that only she and God understood.

I want you to understand that there may be moments in your life when other people will want you to pour when God has called you to save. And vice versa. You have to be so locked in on what God said because you've been called to go deeper. It's more important to be in alignment with God than with man.

There have been times in my life when other people were giving up and tried to talk me out of praying, healing, and forgiving. I'm glad I listened to God. I remember hearing God say that I had to be willing to be who He called me to be in any given season.

When it's all said and done, and the story of our lives are told, heaven won't be impressed with who we knew, what we knew, or what we acquired. Heaven will be impressed by our obedience and surrender, so let it be costly.

When you dare to surrender, it will be unbelievable to other people. It might even be unbelievable to you, but you'll do it with ease because you'll realize none of it was yours anyway. Remember: Your obedience is not about the outcome. It's about showing God that He can trust you with whatever He gives you.

I have a feeling that someone reading this has been saving up for the sake of sidestepping the possibility of lack. That's a scarcity mindset, and you don't even realize it; but you're not trusting God in that area of your life. Maybe it's your voice that you're not sharing with the world. You've been disguising it as you being shy, but you're actually afraid of being rejected again. I'm challenging you to trust Him with your investment and stop trying to be your own savior. Release yourself from engaging in the work of saving yourself. Give Him your pride, voice, and heart and see how He can multiply them.

Lean into the possibility of surrender. It may require a memorial service and a measure of grief. Grief for who you were or still are, but a better version of you exists on the other side of your surrender. When you're ready, ask, "God, what is it that You're asking of me? What is in my life that I've been trying to hang on to? Is it standing in the way of You using me?"

## LAY IT DOWN

I will lean into surrender and give God my pride, voice, and heart, knowing that He can use me.

## 79 Until It's Good

> The land produced vegetation: plants bearing seed according to their kinds and trees bearing fruit with seed in it according to their kinds. And God saw that it was good.
>
> GENESIS 1:12 NIV

**HAVE YOU EVER STRUGGLED WITH BELIEVING THAT GOD** remembers you? He gave you a vision, and it started out going well, but now it looks nothing like He said it would look.

In Genesis 1, God formed the earth and added everything to it. Nothing about His creation was random. Everything was created intentionally. When God finished creating everything, before He rested on the seventh day, He called everything good.

God's creations were patterns set in motion, and at no point did He change His mind about what He was creating. He doesn't just speak something and then move on. The same goes for the vision that He gave you. He didn't speak it to you and deposit the desire in your heart just to leave you empty-handed.

You may be in the midst of struggling, but if it's not good, then He's not finished. God is faithful with good results. Check His track record. Keep working on that word He gave you. There's power in that word, and you've got to work it until it's good.

God has a well-documented pattern: announcement, execution, good. He speaks it until He sees it; and when He sees it, it has got to be good.

The Enemy understands that his best shot of throwing us off our square or disconnecting us from God is to disrupt God's pattern, which ends up creating the Enemy's pattern in the process. In Genesis 3, the Serpent questioned God's announcement to Adam and Eve, which created confusion among them. Today, that confusion sometimes makes us procrastinate or simply do nothing at all, which keeps us from the execution phase of God's pattern. We end up stuck between two patterns—God's pattern and the Enemy's pattern.

Where do we go from here? I hope you will begin to expect the Enemy's cunning ways to be lurking in close proximity to God's pattern. When you expect it, it can't knock you off your square. The intensity of your obedience will be steadier, and you will have a greater expectation for God's power to show up.

Let that expectation become the catalyst for you to tap into the covenant that you have with God. When you are in covenant with God, "no weapon formed against you shall prosper" (Isaiah 54:17). When you are in covenant with God, He will make your enemies your footstool (Psalm 110:1). Being in covenant with God makes "all things work together for good" (Romans 8:28).

Your covenant with God will forever remind you that you're not in this thing on your own. It'll have you trusting His will and refusing to accept anything that hasn't met His standard of good. This doesn't mean it'll always feel prosperous or that the process will always look good, but when you are in covenant with God, you recognize that He doesn't let His words fall to the ground, so you'll do what it takes to follow His lead.

## LAY IT DOWN

Am I willing to be in covenant with God and keep striving toward good?

## 80 Mark the Spot

Jesus heard that they had thrown him out, and when he found him, he said, "Do you believe in the Son of Man?" "Who is he, sir?" the man asked. "Tell me so that I may believe in him." Jesus said, "You have now seen him; in fact, he is the one speaking with you." Then the man said, "Lord, I believe," and he worshiped him.

JOHN 9:35–38 NIV

**DO YOU REMEMBER THE LAST TIME GOD SHOWED UP FOR** you? To some, it may seem simple or mundane for Him to have met you in the shower. For you, no one but God could explain the fact that you have access to warm running water, let alone for it to be in a shower that you get to call yours.

Only you know where God has met you—that low, dark valley and that high, adrenaline-boosting mountaintop. Do you remember what the circumstances were when you cried out for Him? When He comforted, guided, and spoke so clearly to you? Keep those instances in mind. Put pen to paper, recalling every detail that you can remember about them.

Allow those moments to imprint your spirit because you'll need them later. On the day when it seems like His promises won't be fulfilled, on the day when you feel like an imposter in your own life because it all seems too good to be true—remember those places where God met you and held your hand as He navigated you through a season you didn't feel prepared to handle alone.

In John 9, we are told that this man was born blind. The Pharisees questioned how he became healed after having no sight his entire life. He kept telling them that a man, one he'd never met before, had healed him. The Pharisees didn't believe when the man and his parents said he was healed by the Messiah. They threw him out of the synagogue. Jesus found out about him being thrown out, and after a conversation with Jesus, the man became a believer.

Jesus met him when the world around him had decided that he was an undeserving sinner. To them, he entered the world at an unredeemable disadvantage. Can you imagine being told you're not worthy of the healing you've been longing for? Better yet, can you imagine being healed and then those around you questioning the validity of your healing so much that they'd do whatever it took to get you to stop talking about it?

Now imagine limiting the power of your testimony out of fear for what people around you might have to say about it. Those people didn't have to believe like you had to believe for that healing. They didn't have to trust God for an unimaginable breakthrough like you did. If they had, then they'd understand the power and the glory connected to your testimony.

There might also be times when you dare to question whether you should exercise your right to remain silent about what God has done in your life. Maybe you're feeling like a freshman in your faith journey. Maybe the views and opinions of others are louder and more articulate than yours, and that makes you immediately want to shrink or keep quiet.

I want you to be as bold as Jesus was when He reached for the mud to heal that blind man. I want you to remember where you started and where God found you, and look at you now. Slow down for no one. Your healing and faith journey deserve to be shared and experienced.

## LAY IT DOWN

I remember when God showed up for me, and I won't keep silent about my healing and faith journey.

## 81 Context Matters

> I will become even more undignified than this, and I will be humiliated in my own eyes. But by these slave girls you spoke of, I will be held in honor.
>
> 2 SAMUEL 6:22 NIV

**I LOVE THE SOUND OF SOMEONE RECEIVING A BREAK-** through. A spiritual shift is created within me as I hear someone wailing, knowing that a weighty chain has broken off their life. It hasn't always been that way for me. Though I was intrigued by the shouting and praising as a kid and even as a spiritually young adult, I wasn't quite sure that I understood why people needed to be extra with their praise and worship. It took a lot of life experience and spiritual maturation for me to get the full context of why people don't hold back when they praise and worship God.

Just like David's wife, Michal, in 2 Samuel 6:20, when she criticized David for worshiping God freely in public, I had very limited context of what was happening during those Sunday services. Sure, I heard the music, the singers, and the pastor preaching a word, but I didn't know the context behind what was making the people around me shout and speak in tongues. The Holy Spirit wasn't just visiting people for the sake of visitation; those people were praising and worshiping God, using their voices to push back darkness. They were giving God the glory for what was, what is, and what is to come (Revelation 4:8).

Sometimes, especially those of us who are either new to faith or are beginning to take our faith seriously, we may shelter our faith, silencing our praise in hopes of not being judged by others. Even still, there may be critics or questions we are yet trying to answer for ourselves. But I hope you will not lose your voice or fire for God. Outsiders won't have the full context of your encounters with Jesus—and, if I must say, the depths of your relationship with Him may not be any of their business. Find the words to express how God has shown up, been ever-present, and loved you through every storm. I hope no wind in this world is ever strong enough to convince you to stop pressing in and believing in the goodness of God.

David knew that more was in him, a version of himself that Michal never had the opportunity to meet and one he had never introduced to her. Michal didn't have the full context of who David was, yet she determined what his praise should look like. Isn't that something?

There's more to you than what everyone knows, and that's okay. What's known between you and God is what matters the most. God is privy to the full context of who you are, a version that the world may never deserve to know, and He still loves, covers, and guides you. God will protect the details of your life and allow the world to experience only a small portion.

Allow yourself to freely worship Him and know that the depths of your relationship with the Father will continue to expand as life goes on. Trust the time you spend with Him, and allow your life to be an obvious fruit of time well spent.

## LAY IT DOWN

I will worship God freely, giving Him the glory for what was, what is, and what is to come in my life.

## 82 Unfazed by the Dark

> When Jesus heard that John had been put in prison, he withdrew to Galilee. Leaving Nazareth, he went and lived in Capernaum, which was by the lake in the area of Zebulun and Naphtali—to fulfill what was said through the prophet Isaiah: "Land of Zebulun and land of Naphtali, the Way of the Sea, beyond the Jordan, Galilee of the Gentiles—the people living in darkness have seen a great light; on those living in the land of the shadow of death a light has dawned." From that time on Jesus began to preach, "Repent, for the kingdom of heaven has come near."
>
> MATTHEW 4:12–17 NIV

**YOU KNEW A JUICY SECRET WAS ABOUT TO BE REVEALED** when it was preceded by the saying "What goes on in the dark must come out in the light." I've come to realize that this statement also reigns true in our relationship with God and how we partner with Him to face off with the Enemy. In Matthew 4, while fasting for forty days and forty nights, Jesus' private face-off with the Enemy prepared Him for the public attacks He would eventually endure.

Shortly after His fast, Jesus learned about the arrest of John the Baptist, and that changed everything.

You see, there was a plan for Jesus to ease into His ministry as John was meant to prepare the way for Jesus to redeem the fall. John's arrest forced Jesus to face off with enemies who questioned His disruption to their established systems. Jesus' obedience to His Father led Him into the dark unknown with a target on His back, equipped with the belief that God's mission was more significant than the approval of anyone in His way.

I want you to pause for a few minutes before you finish today's devotion. Take a deep breath and think back to a time when you thought you knew God's plan, but things went left. With this in mind, along with what you know about God's character, was God with you in the pivot, or did He leave you hanging? Feel free to insert a praise break right here and journal about your praise report, sis!

After John's death, Jesus didn't have him, but He always had God. I believe it's just as important for you to recognize that God hasn't forsaken you when the plan pivots and takes you through a dark season. The journey may not go as planned, but it must go without ceasing. I want you to trust the spiritual work that you've done privately because it will be the light that navigates you through the dark: "Your word is a lamp for my feet, a light on my path" (Psalm 119:105 NIV).

God's word is a powerful tool meant to guide you. And that's true whether your back is against the wall or you're walking purposely in the direction of the destiny God has assigned to you. The fulfillment of your identity will go through a dark season because the Enemy knows you're a threat to principalities and that you carry God's glory. He wants you to be blinded by the darkness around you, too distracted to acknowledge any bit of flickering light that is God's truth.

What the Enemy hasn't accounted for, but God has, is the fact that you're so deeply rooted in God's love that you're unfazed by the dark. The eyes of your spirit will adjust to the darkness as you walk with God by faith. The Enemy may distract you, but he knows that he can never end what God is doing through you for the kingdom.

For it is already written in heaven.

## LAY IT DOWN

God will go out of His way to guide me through the dark.

## 83 Death by Deception

The LORD God said to the woman, "What is this you have done?" The woman said, "The serpent deceived me, and I ate."

GENESIS 3:13

**EVE IS MY GIRL. YES, THAT EVE. BEFORE YOU GIVE UP ON** her, and me, hear me out.

Have you ever needed God's grace and mercy? Eve was the first one of us to go against what God told us to do, but in my estimation, our girl was also the first one to show us what God's grace and mercy look like.

The Serpent used deception to gain Eve's trust. Isn't that something he's still doing today—planting seeds of deception to change your mind? And because Eve and Adam ate the fruit, they didn't physically die at that moment, but a version of them did. Even though they were disobedient, God still covered them, physically and spiritually.

Eve's actions are proof that no matter the sins we commit, God will still cover us. If you're new to faith, then I want to be the first to warn you: God's covering—His grace and mercy—does not guarantee that the journey will leave you unscathed. God gave Eve a promise in Genesis 3:15–16 that her seed would have dominion over the Enemy, but it would come with some pain, meaning Eve would have to face off with hell to get the job done.

The Enemy used mental deception to change Eve's mind and create sin, which in both Hebrew and Greek means "to miss the mark." Eve's mind was no longer set on God; it was set on whether she could trust God the way she had trusted Him before the Serpent led her astray.

Every day that God gives us breath in our lungs and activity in our brains, we are also given an opportunity not to miss the mark. What does it mean to miss the mark? The division that sin created is standing in the way of your relationship with God. We are more like Eve than many of us would like to admit. We've allowed something or someone to lead us astray, and we trust God less and less. It may not happen every day, but something changed your mind about who God says you are, and before you knew it, you began trusting it more than you trusted God's Word. You've been led astray.

The good news is this: You can never be too far from God. In your most distant form of who God created you to be, He's still giving you grace and mercy. When you feel the most shame or your ego is at its highest, God still loves and cares for you.

When you look back over your life, some situations made you wonder how you got out of them, especially when you weren't living like God was your Father. Let that be proof that He has always been your Father; He was claiming and sparing you even when you were living like you didn't know He existed. The Enemy changed Eve's actions because he changed her mind, but God never changed His mind or actions toward Eve.

## LAY IT DOWN

I am never too far from God, who will never change His loving attitude or actions toward me.

## 84 An Inside Job

> He was wounded for our transgressions, He was bruised for our iniquities; the chastisement for our peace was upon Him, and by His stripes we are healed.
>
> ISAIAH 53:5

**ALL OUR SINS WERE COVERED BY THE BLOOD OF JESUS** when He was nailed to the cross. When there doesn't seem to be a light at the end of the tunnel or when you're not sure how you'll stand up to the giant you're facing, it's going to require the faith to believe that the blood of Jesus over your life still exists. The blood of Jesus still works, and it has the final say.

God's promise to Eve was that her seed would crush the Serpent's head, even with a bruised heel (Genesis 3:15). That promise is the foreshadowing of Jesus coming to defeat death and redeem the fall caused by Adam and Eve in the garden. At that moment, nothing in Eve's life looked like what God said would be accomplished. Sis was fresh off the heels of abandoning what God said and believing the question of the Enemy, yet God trusted her with the coming Savior, who was divine.

Even though Eve never met Jesus, her faith to believe God's promise to her was all she needed to get closer and closer to what He said she could produce. And if we're honest, God's promise was not only about what she would produce; it's about who she had to become on the inside to get the job done. The seed that Eve would initiate the journey that led to the seed that would conquer the Serpent. It took Eve's failure to produce the seed of God's promise. I'm glad that Eve didn't give up on what God told her, even though she didn't live to see it come to fruition.

I know what it's like to have to fight against feelings of

inadequacy. My teenage pregnancy produced shame-based decisions that were poisonous for my spirit. For a decade, I deviated far from God's vision for me. In my mind, there was no way He could use any part of me in His kingdom. But now I know how far He's brought me, so even on my worst days, I will give Him every bit of praise and worship. I trust that if He can do it once, He can do it again and again.

Who you become as a result of the moment that you're standing in has the potential to determine everything. I'm challenging you to give God every bit of shame, inadequacy, doubt, and failure that's been holding you back. In exchange, I want you to start expecting that God will do what He said He would—He will redeem what the locust has eaten (Joel 2:25) so that nothing will be wasted (John 6:12 NIV).

It might take everything you have to keep becoming the woman who will produce the word that God has given you. It may take even more to keep becoming and striving to produce that word when you and the world around you look nothing like what God said. Remember: God never gave up on you. Don't give up on Him or His promises. Keep becoming and believing.

## LAY IT DOWN

I believe the blood of Jesus still works, and His promises to me will come to fruition.

## 85 Believe His Narrative

> You shall receive power when the Holy Spirit has come upon you; and you shall be witnesses to Me in Jerusalem, and in all Judea and Samaria, and to the end of the earth.
>
> ACTS 1:8

**IN THE BEGINNING, WHEN GOD CREATED HUMANITY, THE** Bible says we were made in His image (Genesis 1:27). Being made in the image of God means we were created to have a reflection of God's Spirit dwelling in us. His Spirit is what we need when we're on a mission to accomplish whatever it is God has called us to do.

Once we've come into agreement and vow to reflect God's Spirit, we have to activate what we know to be true about God and what God has said about us. Sometimes we get so caught up in serving or producing for God that we forget to model who we've been serving. Let that marinate. We take on perpetual states of *fear, worry, doubt, shame,* and so many others that are not descriptive of God's image, and I want us to break out of that rhythm because it does not serve God's narrative for us.

I'm reminded of when Jesus was in the garden of Gethsemane and struggling with the tension of His humanity and His Divinity (Luke 22:42–44). He had done all the healing and teaching that He could pack into His three-year ministry on earth, and it was time for Him to surrender to God's narrative once more.

Sometimes we're so busy *reading the Word* that we forget to *become the Word*. We need to be both. You've read the books, listened to the podcasts, gone to the conferences, and found a community of women who are on a similar journey, but when it comes to God's narrative about you, are you modeling it? Not just on the outside through your social media posts, but are you modeling it in your everyday life, especially when it requires intentionality—in the face of anger, accusations, or misunderstandings? Are you a woman of integrity? Are you spreading love and forgiveness?

I will be the last person to say you have to subscribe to being perfect. But I do think we owe it to God to give this life our best shot at being faithful to His Word. As life gets hold of us, we succumb to sin—recall Eve's interaction with the Serpent (Genesis 3). Yet how faithful is God that He so graciously gave us Jesus after Adam and Eve's disobedience in the garden? We, too, have to be faithful when trying to get this thing right because God still wants our lives to model a narrative that will exemplify what is known to be true about God.

I want you to draw a line in the sand. Make the decision today that you are willing to allow God's narrative to be reflected by how you live. You're not reading this book by accident. You have a purpose here, and I want you to own it. God didn't create you just so He could have something to do. He isn't random; He operates with intention. He knows and loves every part of you.

## LAY IT DOWN

I choose to believe God's narrative and reflect it in the way I live.

## 86 Enough, As Is

> He said to Him, "O my Lord, how can I save Israel? Indeed my clan is the weakest in Manasseh, and I am the least in my father's house."
>
> JUDGES 6:15

**I'D BE DOING US BOTH A DISSERVICE IF I PRETENDED AS IF** I am the most confident person at all times. Depending on the area of my life, yes, I feel like I'm that girl. But in a different area of my life, I'm going to need a pep talk in my prayer closet. Our circumstances may be different, but I'm sure we can relate when it comes to wondering if we are enough. I think most people experience this at some point in their lifetimes, wondering if they are enough for the job, the marriage, the friendship, and so forth.

Stepping into a space or a calling that you feel the least qualified for can sometimes feel like you're working from a deficit, even when you know God is involved. I've felt like this from time to time as God has opened doors that I know I could not have opened on my own. I've learned that it's easy to disqualify ourselves based on our history or known capabilities. What's not easy is trying to disqualify anything that's backed by the power of God and led by a person who has surrendered to God.

I'm reminded of this when I think about the story of Gideon in Judges 6. Gideon was in conflict both with his assignment from God, having to go to battle against Israel's oppressors, and with what he thought he knew about himself, which did not align with who God was calling him to be. Gideon started giving God a list of reasons he wasn't the man for the assignment, as if God would say, "You know what? You're right; I'm wrong. My bad. Carry on." Can you imagine? Instead, God, in all His faithfulness, kept His word by showing up to help Gideon and his men win the battle.

God challenged Gideon to surrender the story he had been believing about himself—that he was the weakest and from the smallest tribe. Though there may have been some truth to his perceived shortcomings, Gideon did not fully believe in the power of God's word or His thoughts toward Gideon's capabilities. Like us, Gideon didn't think he was enough to lead a battle that would result in victory, and I think he wasn't too sure that God thought enough of him to actually keep His word, so Gideon asked God for signs that He would keep His word.

How many times has God given you "green flags" of His presence and His thoughts toward you, but you either needed more evidence or simply ignored God altogether? Maybe He told you that He won't abandon you, or He's trusting you to be the type of mother that you didn't have. Whatever it is, I want you to trust that He knows you better than you know yourself. He knows who you are now and what you need to lay down in order to trust that He is with you just as He was with Gideon.

## LAY IT DOWN

I am chosen—who I am right now and who God knows I will become.

## 87 Praying Power

In keeping with your magnificent, unfailing love, please pardon the sins of this people, just as you have forgiven them ever since they left Egypt.

NUMBERS 14:19 NLT

**"GOD QUALIFIES THE CALLED" IS A SAYING I'VE HEARD** repeatedly, and I know it to be true. Prime example: Remember when Moses tried to tell God that he wasn't qualified to lead the children of Israel away from the oppression of the Egyptians? In Exodus 4:10, Moses told God that he was "slow of speech," but God didn't budge on the assignment. Yet in Numbers 14, we see that Moses changed God's mind when he opened his mouth and pleaded on behalf of the people he was called to lead.

This is what prayer is, opening ourselves up to communicate with God. Sometimes it's verbal, but every time it includes our hearts.

I remember when praying out loud was something I avoided like the plague. When someone would ask me to pray for them, without skipping a beat I'd quickly tell them that I'd take their prayer request into my own prayer time. I was being honest, but what I didn't say was that I felt insecure about praying in public. My prayers didn't feel like they opened the windows of heaven. My prayers didn't have any fancy words, and I didn't want to be judged by their simplicity.

How is it that we know prayer changes things, yet we miss numerous opportunities to pray for others because we have the wrong idea of what prayer means? Prayer is about the purity of our hearts as we connect with God. It's not about the words we use or even the outcome that satisfies our desires. Prayer is a way for us to express gratitude and stand in the gap for others.

I've lost count of how many times someone has said they didn't know how to pray or, like me, they compared the effectiveness of their prayers to someone else's whose words seemed more elite. Somewhere along the way, we've subscribed to this idea that prayer has to be loud or sound like the King James Version of the Bible—filled with *thy, thou,* and *art*—to be understood by God. This could not be further from the truth.

I think this train of thought speaks to our view of God and our dynamic with Him. We are God's children, and He is also our friend. When you're in a relationship with God, you'll start to recognize that communication with Him, or prayer, is an exchange, just like when you're speaking to a child or a friend. Praying is as simple as having a conversation with God. You speak and listen, then God speaks and listens too. It's not about how eloquent you can make your prayer sound. It's about how authentic you are in that moment.

I'm not saying you have to grab a microphone or post video proof of your prayers, but I am encouraging you to take your prayers seriously. No matter how simple they are, your prayers have the ability to shift the atmosphere and the trajectory of lives, including your own. Discrediting your prayers is a disservice to the relationship you have with God.

## LAY IT DOWN

My life is the result of God answering someone else's prayer for me.

## 88 Position for Expansion

Then a voice told him, "Get up, Peter. Kill and eat."

ACTS 10:13 NIV

**THERE'S NO SWEETER POSITION THAN TO SURRENDER TO** what only God can call us to do. In Acts 10, Peter received a vision from God that he didn't quite agree with or want to accept. He wrestled with God, questioning what God expected him to do. Peter had to expand his perspective, shifting away from what was forbidden and embracing what was predestined by God.

Expansion requires you to break some rules even though they once worked to your benefit. Peter positioned himself for expansion by doing what the culture said he shouldn't do because God was calling him beyond the culture. Similarly, God is calling us beyond the culture too. Otherwise, we will be married to the culture and how things have always been done. Or we can dare to embrace the mentality of expansion.

God didn't give Peter the vision and then leave. We see in this text that God stuck with him and coached Peter through it, alerting him to what would happen and what steps he would need to take in order to move beyond the limits he had subscribed to. God didn't leave it up to someone else to coach Peter through this moment of expansion; He knew it had to be Him. God gave Peter a word to be released so he could walk in power and trust the vision.

It's time for you to take ownership of the vision God has given you. If you disqualify yourself before you arrive to where God is calling you, then there's a need on the earth that will be left unmet. So it's time to rise and take a step toward what God has predestined and not be limited by the rules of culture. It's time to be released in a way that only God can release you and trust that He will guide you. Trust that He has gone ahead of you and made the space safe for the grace only He has given you to be a solution to the problem only you can solve (Isaiah 45:2).

God is trusting us to lay down what we once abided by because it goes against what He needs from us now. Through the vision God gave Peter in Acts 10, God was calling on a version of Peter that was once rebuked. In John 18, just before Jesus was headed to the cross, Peter attacked one of Jesus' accusers by cutting off his ear. Without command, Peter rose and was ready to fight to keep Jesus from being arrested. But Jesus rebuked Peter in that moment because Peter's actions weren't aligned with the will of God. In Acts 10, however, when God called on this version of Peter, God was giving him permission to be all of who he was for the glory of what God wanted to do at that time.

I don't know what you had to shut down because it didn't work in God's will during a previous season, but I hear God saying that shutting it down back then didn't mean throwing it away. He is about to make a demand on that very thing because it's time.

He's ready to give you strategy. He's ready for your creativity. He's ready for your innovation. He's ready for you to experience a breakthrough. He's ready for you to tap into the power He gave you. It's in you, and the kingdom needs it because when you have a revelation from God, it can change your city, your corner of the world, and your home for the glory of the Lord.

You can be loyal to what you know, or you can be an accomplice to glory. Choose wisely.

## LAY IT DOWN

I choose to rise and take a step toward expansion instead of being limited by the rules of culture.

## 89 Uproot It

"Truly I tell you," Jesus answered, "this very night, before the rooster crows, you will disown me three times."

MATTHEW 26:34 NIV

**IN MATTHEW 26:34, JESUS TOLD PETER THAT HE WOULD** deny him three times, but Peter couldn't fathom it. Instead, Peter declared that he was willing to die with Jesus. Shortly afterward, though, things began to get shaky: Jesus was arrested, and Peter followed Him at a distance.

Peter had walked closely with Jesus in the past. He had faith in Jesus and knew what Jesus represented, but Peter didn't know all of what Jesus knew. Peter hadn't accepted God's plan as Jesus did. The unfolding of Jesus' fate scared Peter into disconnecting from Jesus—first walking at a distance and then denying having walked with Jesus at all.

Prior to the denials, in Matthew 16:13–20, Peter declared boldly that Jesus was the Messiah. Peter was no different from you and me. We may not have verbally denied our faith in Jesus or lied to say we haven't been in His presence, but our actions have certainly spoken louder than our words ever could: The refusal to see good after we've been wronged. Our willingness to become a cynic, disconnected from hope, love, and joy. The way we worship our problems instead of His promises. Our constant worry instead of the faith to trust that God's plan is still good no matter the outcome.

The habits we develop matter. Our habits should reflect what we believe. Our inclinations, maturing over time, are key indicators of the health of our relationship with God.

Take inventory of what's inside you that no longer serves you.

When you do, you'll begin to figure out the root cause of the bitterness that has poisoned your heart and limited your ability to experience unconditional joy. Get to the root of what has been encouraging you to deny Jesus. Is it the fear of having to trust His plan? In John 18, Peter saw what was happening to Jesus and feared it would be his fate too. That's why we have to trust the plan of God, not an outcome. When we have more faith in an outcome, we lose sight of the fact that God's will is more purposeful than our desired outcome.

Notice that in Matthew 26:34, Jesus told Peter the exact number of times he would deny Him: "You will disown Me three times" (NIV). Peter needed to get those denials out of the way for many reasons. Confronting what was inside him meant he could make room for what needed to be inside him—the truth that he was human and capable of having his core beliefs stripped away when things got shaky. Peter was on the front line of spreading the gospel, a target for attacks. He needed to know that his faith would be tested and that he would need to stand firm.

Like Peter, your faith will take hits, become bruised, and require a recentering. Be prepared for it to happen, and have a plan for how you'll respond when it comes—seek God's thoughts and wisdom, recognize the feelings that are springing forth within you, and be mindful of what your actions and words are saying about your faith in God's plan. Faith is a muscle that gets stronger as it is exercised and has the ability to heal after it is bruised.

## LAY IT DOWN

I know that someday my faith will be tested, and I will need to stand firm.

## 90 Unfiltered

"Before I formed you in the womb I knew you; before you were born I sanctified you; I ordained you a prophet to the nations." Then said I: "Ah, Lord God! Behold, I cannot speak, for I am a youth."

JEREMIAH 1:5–6

**IN JEREMIAH 1:5, GOD TOLD JEREMIAH THAT HE KNEW HIM** better than Jeremiah knew himself. God told Jeremiah that just as he had been dependent on his mother in her womb, He knew that humanity would be dependent on Jeremiah's prophecies. Before Jeremiah could form sentences or had submitted his life to believing in God, God knew that Jeremiah had a gift of prophesy that would echo across the generations.

I want to make sure we understand this because the way Jeremiah responded to God's calling is often an afterthought, or not even discussed, when this passage is quoted. Jeremiah's response, telling God that he could not speak—though he was actually speaking—and that he was a youth, was his way of trying to discredit who God was calling him up to be.

Jeremiah's response took God's word and filtered it through the context of his own worldview. He couldn't fathom that, at his young age and with his youthful thought patterns, he could be a prophet. Jeremiah had to make a decision: Did he want to continue to filter his relationship with God through his limited worldview, or did he want to submit to the word that God had given him and shed every bit of logic that defied what God had said?

Maybe God is calling you to forgive over and over again, but your humanity encourages you to be stubborn because it feels safer. Maybe God is calling you to raise your child differently, but prominent voices in your family are imploring that the one-size-fits-all style of parenting they used will work for you too. Maybe God is calling you to speak up, but your worldview has celebrated the silence and oppression of women, so it scares you to share something you know will dismantle systems and shift the culture around you.

God sent a word to Jeremiah, and He is sending a word to us that will cut up the limiting filter of our worldview. God's word is a sword that cuts up our internal oppositions—insecurities, inadequacies, and egotistical issues. We have to use God's word as a reframing tool and allow it to expand our perspectives.

When God forms a version of us that we can't fathom becoming, we have to dig deeper and reframe our perspectives because we don't want to compromise God's word. When we water down or edit a word God has given us, we limit the glory that is connected to that word. Instead of seeing the word as a way that God is drawing you out of your comfort zone, reframe it to see it as a way that God is using you as a vessel to draw people closer to Him. It's not about making your name great; it's about the glory connected to the vessel God is using, and it happens to be you.

When God is calling us to expand our way of thinking or capacity, sometimes our greatest threat is the filter of our lived experiences. We become jaded, dry, and willing to be placed in a box, when God is calling us to reframe with His limitless perspective. Jeremiah thought he was too young to be used by God, but God knew that age was no match to what He could do. You may be underdeveloped now, but God will develop and grow you up internally for where He is taking you.

## LAY IT DOWN

God is calling me to expand my capacity and reframe my experiences with His limitless perspective.

## 91 Trust the Game Plan

Though He slay me, yet will I trust Him. Even so, I will defend my own ways before Him.

JOB 13:15

**GROWING UP IN DALLAS, TEXAS, IT WAS EASY FOR ME TO** become a fan of our hometown professional sports teams. Let me say, I was not a sports girlie. I didn't play sports and I barely watched, but I am familiar with a bit of the lingo. For instance, I know that starters on a team are usually the best players to match up offensively and defensively against their opponents. This methodology also applies to our position in the kingdom.

As we read the story of Job in the Bible, we see that if God was the coach, then Job was a starter. God knows of the ways in which the Enemy will game-plan against us. He allowed the Enemy to attack Job's possessions, knowing that none of the attacks would give the Enemy the victory he was pursuing: getting Job to stop trusting God's faithfulness and ultimately crushing Job's faith.

The Enemy tries to steal, kill, and destroy (John 10:10). He has no new ways to attack us but uses these three tactics in every area of our lives. God knows it and so do we, yet the Enemy tends to succeed in distracting us from God's plan for our lives. That's why we should strive to live with the perspective of Job, who said, "Though He slay me, yet will I trust Him" (Job 13:15). When we, like Job, are standing and being bold in our faith, I believe we will begin to see the Enemy's tricks as no more than smoke and mirrors.

Don't get me wrong: The Enemy's attacks are real, and they're strong enough to take us out. I want you to be spiritually prepared for them, being able to identify them as valid threats and partnering with God to overcome what's in your way. That game plan is called spiritual maturity. It takes time to learn it and be effective with it, but it's not beyond you.

Scripture tells us over and over that God will be with us in the face of battles that appear to be bigger than we are. A practical tool we can take with us is believing that God is in the fight with us. It's something we tend to agree with in hindsight once it has all worked out, but what if we believed and moved like we knew God is with us at the beginning and in the middle of a battle?

Trusting that God will be with you is very similar to the process of trusting the outcome of a new recipe. You may be familiar with the ingredients, but since it's the first time you're using them to achieve a particular outcome, you may be wondering if they will mix well. There's only one way to know: Try it.

Trusting God may not be new for you, but adding to the depth of your trust in Him may feel new. Why wouldn't it? It's new for you to need to trust God on that level, so you may have some hesitation with handing that need over. That is fair, but don't stay there.

Trust God's game plan. His word never fails. He said He will be with us. We can trust Him.

## LAY IT DOWN

I will be prepared for the Enemy's attacks in my life when I trust God's game plan.

## 92 Unsuspected Partner

I no longer call you servants. . . . Instead, I have called you friends, for everything that I learned from my Father I have made known to you.

JOHN 15:15 NIV

**CULTURE IS FILLED WITH COLLOQUIALISMS THAT CELE-** brate the solitary individual—*self-made, solo dolo,* and *trust no one,* to name a few. In the rare instances that friendships are celebrated, "no new friends" is a phrase often announced as a way to keep that space under lock and key.

Throughout Scripture, we see that even when people have moments of solitude, community is celebrated the most: Mary the mother of Jesus had Elizabeth, Ruth had Naomi, and Martha had her sister, Mary. Rahab looked out for the spies. Esther had her cousin Mordecai. Paul had Silas. Jesus had the disciples. Women who were cultural outcasts—such as the woman with the issue of blood and the woman at the well—ended up in community with Jesus, even if for a brief moment.

Even when you and I are physically alone, we have the Holy Trinity—the Father, the Son, and the Holy Spirit. Being in community with others is our birthright. During the time you're spending with Jesus, whether intentionally or randomly, you're nurturing that partnership and strengthening its bond. You are solidifying the importance of community and what it means to be in an intimate relationship with someone other than yourself.

I don't want to pretend like finding a healthy core group of friends is simple. I know that finding like-minded friends can be difficult, but I believe the rewards are worth putting in the effort. It may be awkward and well beyond your comfort zone, but that's okay. There's something about having at least one or two people who understand you and see you better than you see yourself. Like God does, your friends call you higher, don't let you sell yourself short, and love you through the hard stuff.

I'm an introvert, and small talk isn't really my thing. I've found community through childhood relationships and those that I've nurtured through work situations. I'm also a girl's girl, so giving a compliment is something I'm always a fan of as a conversation starter. I mean, don't you tend to let your guard down when another woman tells you how fly your shoes are, asks about your makeup or skincare routine, or asks what your scent combo is?

As you're evolving, there are seasons when you need solitude, when you need to take a deep breath and get away from the loud noises of the world. The right friends will understand this, and they will hold space for you until you return. When God sends you the friends you need to help hold you up, I pray you don't miss out on these unsuspecting partners. Whether for a season or a lifetime, I hope your heart remains open to sisterhood. Sisterhood is a village of support cultivated by God.

### LAY IT DOWN

Although I need seasons of solitude, I will solidify the importance of community by finding a healthy core group of friends.

## 93 Make the Decision

> Behold, I give you the authority to trample on serpents and scorpions, and over all the power of the enemy, and nothing shall by any means hurt you.
>
> LUKE 10:19

**WHAT IF YOU WERE GOD'S ONLY OPTION? MAYBE YOU'RE** standing on the shoulders of giants, and God has ordained you to continue a legacy paved before you while also trusting you to create a new lane. It doesn't even have to be something so lofty and big. Maybe He has given you the vision for a book or a nonprofit, or maybe He's allowing motherhood to stretch you or calling you to the challenge of changing how you communicate. That thing, that idea that's been pulling at you—would you continue to talk yourself out of it if you knew for sure that your life, and the lives of others, depended on you making the decision to get it done?

These are real questions to sit with. Let them marinate in your mind, heart, and spirit. Begin living like you believe the power God has granted you access to is the key to unlocking the power that someone holds. The Enemy already knows it, and God knows it, but I need you to know it.

And you've got to be so sure about your vision that nothing will deter you from getting it done. It doesn't matter how long it takes or who is or isn't with you from start to finish, sis; it only matters that as long as your mind is set on God, you make the decision. The "big girl" decision. The one that says, "I'm not going to let fear talk me out of this. I'm not going to let nervousness tell me that I'm inadequate. I'm not going to let my lack of an up-close blueprint tell me that because I don't know all the steps, then I can't take a step in the direction of where God is calling me."

It's time to abandon what once made you comfortable, because being comfortable isn't going to serve you in a season when a critical decision must be made. Know the difference between comfort and contentment. To be content is to know that what you have, who you are, and what you're doing has value and is enough, though you're striving to evolve.

I'm not talking about material things; that's a low-level way of thinking. I'm talking about what you have inside you: Can you forgive again? Can you love again? Who have you become? Are you a woman of integrity? What are you doing to expand the kingdom? Are you serving others? Are you helping another woman keep her crown intact? Or are you comfortable with living in a silo and being ineffective in the kingdom? To be comfortable is to be in agreement with being stagnant and accepting limitations. There's little to no growth in comfort. Make the decision to stretch beyond being comfortable.

Are you willing to get on the front line and stand up to the life-shifting decision that you need to make as if your life depends on it? It is going to require you to live in complete surrender and obedience. A life so surrendered to God that you recognize and honor the power you hold over the Enemy. Obedience will become your act of resistance.

## LAY IT DOWN

I will set my mind on where God is sending me, and I'm going to need His power to get it done.

## 94 Power over the Enemy

So the Lord God said to the serpent: "Because you have done this, you are cursed more than all cattle, and more than every beast of the field; on your belly you shall go, and you shall eat dust all the days of your life. And I will put enmity between you and the woman, and between your seed and her Seed; He shall bruise your head, and you shall bruise His heel."

GENESIS 3:14–15

**SO OFTEN WE TALK ABOUT GENERATIONAL CURSES AND** blessings, but not often enough do we acknowledge the promises of God connected to them. We joke about what we'd say to Eve because of the decision she made, but we don't give her enough credit for her belief in having power over the Enemy. The faith that Eve later showed in the promise of this power is truly a generational blessing.

After the fall in the garden of Eden, Eve had every reason to squander away her life. By all accounts, she had messed it up for all humanity. Imagine how embarrassed she must have been at showing distrust in God and becoming the reason she and her husband were kicked out of the garden. She could have built a home in the center of her humiliation and stayed there, a victim of the consequences of her own decision, not even acknowledging the promise that God had given her. But when God made a connection that her seed would reverse the curse of eating from the fruit, Eve fought through whatever emotions and defeat she may have felt. She gave birth to Cain and Abel, and well, we know how that went. But then through having Seth, she hit the ground running into the direction that rerouted our paths.

At face value, we all started at a deficit because of a decision that Adam and Eve made; our lives began with a curse that started in the garden. We have to start reframing this and embrace the fact that we were also given a promise that God would defeat the Enemy; we were born victorious before we ever knew we'd be in a fight.

I can't count the number of times I've experienced embarrassing public failures or had my ill-advised decisions negatively impact the lives of other people. Can you? This is why Eve is such a game changer. She didn't mind taking humiliation and failure along for her journey toward redemption.

Think about an ill-advised or immature decision you made that either drastically changed your life or could have, and it will make you empathize with Eve. Now think about the work it took for Eve, and yourself, to overcome that mistake. Consider how God spared your life and the lives of others because of your decision. God could have let Adam and Eve die. He could've let your dream, your goals, or you die, but He didn't. Eve took a chance by testing forbidden waters, and she almost drowned. God had other plans in mind, but Eve had to rise to the occasion to see God's plan come to life.

This applies to us. You are not your worst mistake. You are still a citizen of heaven and loved by God. Every day, I want you to hit the ground running into the direction of your healing, reconciliation, and redemption. This may look like forgiving yourself for not doing better even when you knew better. Or maybe it's fasting from things that distract you from God's Word or intentionally working toward executing something that God gave you. Ask God and let Him guide you. Victory is yours.

## LAY IT DOWN

I am not my worst decision or mistake; I'm a citizen of heaven and loved by God, who guides me to victory.

## 95 Rough Draft

Your eyes saw my substance, being yet unformed. And in Your book they all were written, the days fashioned for me, when as yet there were none of them.

PSALM 139:16

**IF WE WERE HAVING A MENTORING MOMENT AND I SAID,** "God loves you, and He will never forsake you," would you believe me if your life had a few fires that needed to be put out? If not, then I want you to get to a point where you believe that God's promises are especially true for you when what you are experiencing doesn't exactly match what He said.

Hebrews 12:2 says God is "the author and the finisher of our faith," meaning it all starts and ends with God. The New International Version translates "author" and "finisher" as "pioneer" and "perfecter," respectively. This should tell you that if what you see in your life today doesn't quite align with what He said, then you're in the middle of your story and He has yet to perfect it. You're still in the rough draft stages as God, the ultimate editor with the final say, will make revision after revision until the story is exactly as He said it would be. Not how your parents said it, now how statistics projected it, and not how your environment tried to shift it. God has the final say.

What happens when we can't receive God's story because of what we believe about our stories? I think this is when we toe the line of becoming like the children of Israel, the people who were led out of captivity by Moses. Their journey from Egypt to the promised land, spanning four decades, should have been complete in about two weeks. But their lack of faith in God's plan, disobedience, and desire to take matters into their own hands came at a great cost. God cursed them to wander in the wilderness for forty years because they lacked faith, and many of them did not make it to the land that God had promised them.

Our job is to live out the story He wrote for us. Just like the Israelites, the territory is yours. The victory is yours. Wholeness is yours. You have to believe it though. Who do you have to become to harness this belief? What do you have to lay down to believe that God's promises are inherently yours? God didn't forget about you; He's waiting for you to surrender to believing the good things He's promised you.

Remember when God was deep in His creation of the world, creating day and night, the animals and Adam? Everything eventually became good in God's sight before He moved on to the next part of creation. The same applies to your story. You're here with a life to be lived, which means God is using His time wisely to make it good. Stay in your lane and trust your journey.

Just before Scripture says "God is the author and finisher of our faith" (Hebrews 12:2), there's a command we must adhere to: Fix your eyes on Jesus (NIV). This verse doesn't say look at your circumstances or survey what God is doing for others. Yes, you have to be aware of your situation, and yes, sometimes it's good to know God is still working things out for others because it can give you hope when you're running low. But that doesn't mean you begin to worship your issues or develop jealousy for the highs that others are experiencing. Be mindful of where your mind goes when you're observing your circumstances and the blessings that God has given to others. Surrender to being a rough draft who is willing to undergo constant revisions.

## LAY IT DOWN

God has written the story of my life, and He is using His time wisely to make it good.

## 96 God's Flexibility

"For my thoughts are not your thoughts, neither are your ways my ways," declares the Lord.

ISAIAH 55:8 NIV

**HAVE YOU EVER EXPERIENCED A RESTRUCTURE IN A** work environment? Afterward, having a well-defined role and being provided with clear expectations, you probably found yourself being more deliberate about how you completed your tasks because some things were no longer expected of you, and new job functions were now yours to complete.

I recently learned about cognitive flexibility, which is our ability to appropriately adapt our behavior to an environment as it changes. This is critical because when we understand that the end goal remains achievable regardless of the role we play along the way, we have to be willing to change our routine because our future success depends on it. It is important to remember that your goal is only as good as your routine.

Navigating a restructuring can be tricky. New behaviors in familiar environments often breed discomfort because of your expectations. This also happens in our relationship with God. Our expectations of God have to be flexible. Yes, He is the same God as your ancestors declared Him to be—faithful and consistent—but the ways in which He shows up in your life may change every time you experience Him. Unchanged expectations place God in a box and limit your ability to experience His fullness.

When Isaiah 55:8 says that our thoughts are not His thoughts, it's true. While we want our thoughts to reflect that we are in relationship with God, His ways are expansive, unique, and diverse. It is impossible to know exactly how God perceives a situation or the details of how and when He will make His presence known. We have to be willing to be flexible in how we allow our minds to shape our perspectives of how God moves. We may think we're abandoned when God doesn't show up according to our desired timeline, but if we take a look around, we'll see that God never left us. He protected us from the worst and still provided for us when we gave Him our least.

I don't want you to be married to stale faith or locked in on expecting God to be repetitive in how He operates so that you miss what God is doing now. Every day, be intentional about breaking away from your old routine of how you expect God to show up. Instead, embrace that God will still show up but in a fresh, new way. Remind yourself that God will go beyond what you can even comprehend, so release Him of the logical expectations you have of Him (Ephesians 3:20). This earthly experience all started as a miracle. Confining God to what's logical is detrimental to your spiritual growth.

Letting go of the routine expectations of who you think God is will introduce you to how strategic God is. Honestly believing that God can be sitting with you in this very moment while also ahead of you and waiting for you to catch up with Him requires a level of flexibility that I want you to have in your relationship with Him. Let go and let God, but for real this time.

## LAY IT DOWN

I release my logical expectations of God, believing that He will show up in a fresh, new way.

## 97 Powerful Confrontation

> But the angel of the Lord said to Elijah the Tishbite, "Go up and meet the messengers of the king of Samaria and ask them, 'Is it because there is no God in Israel that you are going off to consult Baal-Zebub, the god of Ekron?'"
>
> 2 KINGS 1:3 NIV

**I WANT TO GIVE YOU A LITTLE BACKSTORY FOR THIS TEXT** so you can fully understand why it's so good! Ahaziah, the king of Samaria, had fallen and eventually became ill. He sent some messengers to consult with Baal-Zebub, the enemy and a false god. The prophet Elijah was sent by the angel of the Lord to confront the king, who was a nonbeliever in search of an answer from someone who wasn't equipped to accurately respond.

The king was desperate for an answer about his future, but he didn't ask the One who gave him life. Instead, when he was most vulnerable and looking for hope, he put his trust in the enemy. I'm inclined to ask you if this sounds familiar, but I have a feeling I know the answer. The king isn't the only person who's ever turned their back on God and put faith in someone or something that meant them no good.

Think about the heartbreak that led you to drinking. Or what about the neglect that pointed you in the direction of drugs? I'm not judging you or pointing my finger; I've been in the same rough spots too. It took a rude awakening for me, and the king, to realize that God stands on business. God told Elijah that the king's plan to consult the enemy, Baal-Zebub, would be the cause of his death, and so it was.

I don't want this for you. I know it's hard to turn away from your vices—self-sabotage, substance abuse, self-harm, and the list goes on—and God knows it too. Every day that He gives you a beating heart and a mind that has the ability to make a decision, that's another day for you to make power moves toward choosing Him over consulting with Baal-Zebub.

Power moves cause confrontation. We need the confrontation to happen because it breaks up systems. The king of Samaria needed Elijah to confront him on God's behalf for him to understand that God is real. That confrontation made the king stand face-to-face with his decision and who God is.

For Elijah, in this instance, confrontation created influence. For us, it's a reminder that when we're served with a moment of confrontation, we should desire for it to be a moment of value to highlight the kingdom. Confrontation happens in our everyday lives—at work, in our relationships, and within ourselves. Whatever we're called to confront, may we do it in a way that is led by the fruit of the Spirit (Galatians 5:22–23) and creates unimaginable healing for everyone involved.

Take the limits off what it means to be in conflict. If we go through life without confrontation, then we are agreeing never to confront the things that desperately need to be changed; we are in agreement with the status quo and silently proclaiming that all is well. But solutions are birthed from our ability to effectively navigate confrontation.

## LAY IT DOWN

Whatever I'm called to confront, may I do it in a way that is led by the fruit of the Spirit and creates healing for everyone involved.

## 98 Who Are You?

> The king asked them, "What kind of man was it who came to meet you and told you this?"
>
> 2 KINGS 1:7 NIV

**IN 2 KINGS 1, WE SEE THAT THE MESSENGERS OF AHAZIAH,** the king of Samaria, were on the way to consult with Baal-Zebub, the enemy and a false god, when the prophet Elijah stopped them. The messengers were sent back to tell the king of Samaria what God had told Elijah: "Is it because there is no God in Israel that you are going off to consult Baal-Zebub, the god of Ekron?" (v. 3 NIV). The messengers must have returned to the king sooner than he had anticipated because he asked why they had returned. They told him about Elijah's interference in their mission and the message he'd given them.

How is it that Elijah, a prophet, had more power and authority over the king's messengers than the king had over them? Something in me can't shake the fact that a word from God is what changed their mind about the plans they'd received from their king. They didn't fear the wrath of the king or any repercussions that may have come. They knew the word that God gave them through Elijah was more important than the danger of not following the king's order.

There will be times when you have a word from God that changes every plan you had. You will abide by it with little to no questions. It won't make sense to others, but the way it hits your spirit is all the sense and confirmation you will need. I hope you will lean into those moments and write them down so that you can access them when you're running low on trusting what God told you.

The messengers didn't even ask for Elijah's name; they were only able to describe his outward appearance, and the king knew who he was. This tells me that Elijah had an unforgettable presence. There's something about you that stands out too. Maybe it's how you serve others or how welcoming your spirit is. There's something about you that has others wondering, *Who are you?* They won't have to wonder for long because soon they will begin to recognize that you are the daughter of the Most High.

I want you to begin asking yourself, *Who am I?* and find scriptures to support who God says you are. The answer to every question you have about yourself—who you are, why you were created, and the list goes on—can be found in God's Word. "Seek, and you will find," Jesus said in Matthew 7:7. Notice that He didn't say *might* but *will*. What God knows about you is readily available to you, so the next time someone asks, "Who do you think you are?" you'll be able to confidently tell them who God says you are. I want you to speak God's Word when someone questions your presence, knowing that God's power resides in you and that you have authority in every space He sends you. You are evolving beautifully into the woman God always knew you would become. Rise to every occasion and own who you are.

## LAY IT DOWN

I am a daughter of the Most High, confident that God's power resides in me and that I have authority in every space He sends me.

## 99  Two Things Can Be True

> You intended to harm me, but God intended it for good to accomplish what is now being done, the saving of many lives.
>
> GENESIS 50:20 NIV

**I'VE FOUND THAT FOR MANY PEOPLE, AFTER THEY DEDI-** cate themselves to live for Christ, they are surprised when their life is not easy. We are probably more open to the Enemy's foolishness when we are keenly aware of God's power and His faithfulness. The Enemy knows God is with us. Simultaneously, the Enemy is working to steal that belief and get us to turn away from God.

I want you to think back to an experience that reminds you of not being forgotten by God. If you dive a little deeper, are you able to acknowledge that there was also a moment where you wondered why the Enemy knew your name? There is something powerful about knowing that two intentions can be at work at the same time.

In the book of Genesis, we see that Joseph grew up knowing what it felt like to have favor from his father, Jacob. Eventually, that favor became seedlings from which jealousy grew within his brothers, who ended up selling Joseph into slavery. He was later falsely accused and spent some time in prison. Joseph couldn't catch a break, having over a decade of his life taken from him because of what an adversary meant for evil. There was an opportunity for Joseph to be released from his unjust prison sentence, but man had forgotten about him. All along, God's favor remained with Joseph, as He kept reminding Joseph that He was with him and hadn't forgotten about him.

There will be times when man will do the exact opposite of

what God does for us. In those moments, we question God and His plan or His faithfulness. Joseph continued to believe in the goodness of God, even when his life was the most difficult. As we mature in our faith, recognizing that attacks will come, I hope we remember that just as God was with Joseph, He is with us too. Even in situations that Joseph didn't want to be in, enslaved and imprisoned, Scripture says, "The Lord was with Joseph and gave him success in whatever he did" (Genesis 39:23 niv).

Joseph embodied what Paul later told the believers in Galatia about not getting weary in well-doing. He said, "Let us not become weary in doing good, for at the proper time we will reap a harvest if we do not give up" (Galatians 6:9 niv). Joseph trusted God, and he continued to do good even when others mistreated him. Joseph rose in power and eventually had the chance to help his brothers, the ones who had sold him into slavery. He could have sought revenge by turning his back on them. Instead, Joseph covered his brothers' needs and forgave them.

Two things will be true: Wrongdoing will come to you many times in your life, and God will be with you every time. Remember Joseph's tales and remember your own. Ask God, "What would You have me do in this situation?" You will have the chance to choose between righteousness and revenge, faith or hopelessness. Be wise in your choices.

## LAY IT DOWN

I can choose to do good, even when others mistreat me, because God is with me always.

## 100 Finish Strong

I have fought the good fight, I have finished the race, I have kept the faith.

2 TIMOTHY 4:7

**THE ONLY WAY ANY OF US CAN TRULY STAY POWERFUL IN** the way that matters the most is to stay connected to the all-powerful, all-knowing, and ever-present God. We're the only thing God has created that runs the risk of living without the original power God intended us to possess. The sun, ocean, moon, and stars still take their place each morning and evening. Some days their brightness is more luminous than others. In some seasons they're hardly detectable at all, but never do they cease to have power. I want you to know that staying power will look different from season to season.

Staying power is about having faith that believes where you are, no matter how old or irrelevant it may seem, is not out of God's sight and can still be used for His plan.

When we make the destination of staying power about living authentically and actively seeking God's heart and perspective on our truth, it allows us to lean in to how He may transform us. If you're going to finish strong at anything, you must stay connected to the ultimate Finisher.

I don't know about you, but I don't want to finish as a hero in everyone else's eyes but a failure at maximizing who God knew I could be. If the metrics of other people's opinions and thoughts are how you determine whether or not you're powerful, you'll run the risk of making acceptance and validation from others your finish line. Feedback without God as your filter can damage your soul and thwart your destiny. I have to remind myself to not be so focused on the metrics and be more sensitive to when God is challenging me to remember that who I am is more important than what I can offer.

Just in case finishing strong for you has always been about measuring quantifiable outcomes or receiving feedback from those you're in relationship with, I want you to consider something. If there were no report to review and the mouths that surrounded you were muted, how would you know in your soul that you finished strong? As a parent, partner, friend, sibling, child, or colleague, how would you know? When life inevitably turns the page from one role to the next, how will you know that you've walked away with power from that stage as opposed to losing your power in the transition?

Anytime you finish with a lesson that helps you see yourself more clearly and trust God more completely, you have finished strong. You're probably thinking about how many finishes resulted in a lesson that holds power. Guess what? Even if you have unfinished business from transitions that left you feeling powerless, know that revenge is not a medium for power—it's an abuse of it—but perspective is.

Trusting that doing it the way God has ordered, no matter how unique, is the only path to ultimate freedom. Find your confidence to be authentic. Trust that you can effect change. Don't you dare get stuck in stagnancy, and do all you can to ask for help when you've gone astray. Keep your heart open to the impossible, and trust that you have the endurance to withstand the inevitable fears that come.

## LAY IT DOWN

It's not too late to find the lesson and discover the strength to live again.

## About the Author

**SARAH JAKES ROBERTS IS A *NEW YORK TIMES* BESTSELL-**ing author, speaker, entrepreneur, and philanthropist. She is the founder of Woman Evolve, a multimedia platform that provides women with the tools, support, and encouragement necessary to make positive and lasting changes. Through various resources such as digital and live events, books, podcasts, and online content, Woman Evolve seeks to address the holistic needs of women and empower them to lead fulfilling and impactful lives.

Alongside her husband, Touré Roberts, she serves as an assistant pastor at The Potter's House of Dallas. Her messages spread throughout the world, defying cultural, religious, gender, and socioeconomic boundaries. With her down-to-earth personality, contemporary style, and revelatory messages, there's no question why TIME100 Next named her an emerging thought leader for this generation.

## DOES THE PRESSURE TO DO MORE, BE MORE, AND ACHIEVE MORE LEAVE YOU FEELING POWERLESS?

In *Staying Power*, global ministry leader and *New York Times* bestselling author Sarah Jakes Roberts challenges you to let go of others' expectations and embrace the calling God has for you—with the power only He can give.

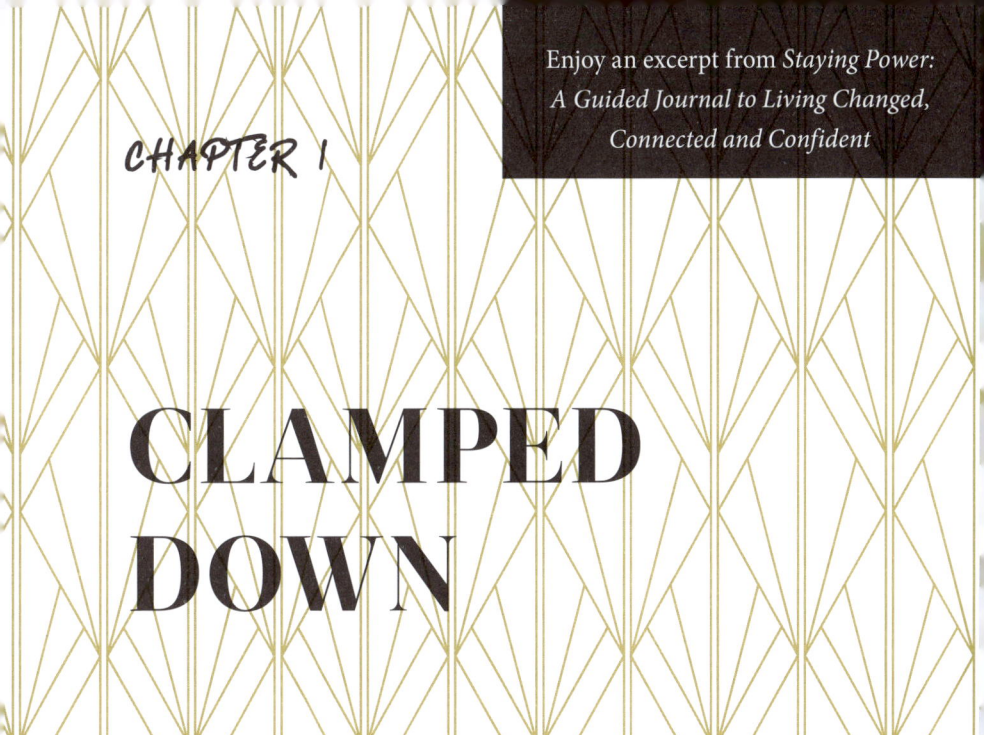

# CHAPTER 1

*Enjoy an excerpt from Staying Power: A Guided Journal to Living Changed, Connected and Confident*

# CLAMPED DOWN

**LET US LAY ASIDE EVERY WEIGHT, AND THE SIN WHICH SO EASILY ENSNARES US, AND LET US RUN WITH ENDURANCE THE RACE THAT IS SET BEFORE US.**

**HEBREWS 12:1**

A few months into living in our home, my husband and I hopped into bed after a long day. We were ready to unwind with an episode of our favorite show. I grabbed the remote and pointed it at the television. Nothing happened. Through a process of elimination, I could confidently say the problem wasn't the remote, and it wasn't the outlet. The problem was actually inside the television.

What was so interesting about the TV no longer working was not that it lacked power. The power was flowing, but there was something internally keeping the TV from converting the power into function.

If you've ever been in an environment where you've felt incapable of demonstrating confidence, you may be more like the busted TV than you realize. Fortunately, there's a secret advantage to being like that television that should give you more of a sense of relief than exasperation. The television had access to power. Since the issue was with the device, our focus could be on converting the power it had access to into power to function in the way it was designed to function.

Your breath is evidence that power is still accessible to you. If you have breath, you have access. Right now, in this very moment, power from God is on and flowing in your direction.

## RELEASE THE PRESSURE

No matter how you feel right now, you're not irreparably broken, incapable, or inadequate. The ultimate limitation you're experiencing is the result of constant internal and external pressure to conform, stay silent, perform, or achieve. When that pressure is never released, it eventually ends up having more power to stop you than you have to break free from it.

Right now, in this very moment, power from God is on and flowing in your direction.

**Name an area of your life where you're feeling pressure to:**

**Conform**

_____

_____

_____

_____

_____


**Stay silent**

_____

_____

_____

_____

_____

**Perform**

_____

_____

_____

_____

_____

**Achieve**

_____

_____

_____

_____

Releasing the pressure and learning to be powerful does not have to come at the expense of trampling on opportunities and connections you value. You can walk in power, love, humility, and kindness all at the same time. Jesus is a beautiful example of this truth. It's essential that you become discontent with the way things are and hungry for what could be so we can work together to get you to the most powerful you.

*You're going to break through what has limited you. . . . You're a force in the making.*

Are you discontent with the way things are? Take a moment to jot down the things you long to see change.

_____

_____

_____

_____

_____

You're going to break through what has limited you—armed with the power to never be limited again. You're a force in the making.

## COURAGEOUSLY AUTHENTIC

A wide range of culprits zap our power. Here are a few signs that can indicate you're experiencing a loss of power. Check the circles for the ones you can relate to:

- ○ You find yourself habitually conforming to ideas that sharply contrast with what you really want or believe.
- ○ You feel frustrated when asked to fulfill obligations that you set the precedent to complete.

- You feel resentful at other people's ability to freely express themselves.
- You find yourself overreacting to trivial issues.
- You feel a constant longing and discontentment.
- You choose appeasing others over advocating for yourself.
- You feel trapped inside your life, regardless of how many things should be sources of joy.
- You feel annoyed when people speak, especially incorrectly, on your behalf or about you in your presence.

Now is not the time to lament over the power you've lost. This is an opportunity to acknowledge and accept that the loss of power is a gift. It makes space for you to seek a connection to our all-powerful God who refills, restores, and refuels you in the place where you experienced loss. The dilemma then is not how to take up space and make demands on ourselves and others so our authentic selves can come back to life. Instead, our journeys revolve around us returning to an uninhibited version of ourselves that is not in a struggle for power because we recognize our authenticity *is* power.

## REFLECT ON YOUR FEARS

We can't determine the external variables that have clamped you down until you're willing to acknowledge the fears you think change will bring. Your fears have the power to keep you stuck, but the beginning of disarming that fear is when you dare to confront it with intention.

As much as I'd like you to be able to dive right in to being your most confident, powerful self, I also know lasting change takes time. Taking time to reflect is how we will lay the foundation.

**What are you afraid will happen if the power you long for becomes the power you embody?**

_____

_____

_____

**Reflect on a powerless moment you experienced in your day. What would choosing power have looked like?**

_____

_____

_____

Let's begin the journey where you work on realigning your focus, thoughts, and energy to your authenticity and allowing it all to overflow into your purpose, personal community, and ambitions. For now this work is an inside job between you and God.